Encore
Secrets of Serial Entrepreneurship

DEREK SAUDER

Copyright © 2015 Derek Sauder

All rights reserved.

ISBN:1505636663
ISBN-13:978-1505636666

CONTENTS

Foreword vii
Preface 1
Introduction 3

Part 1 – Business Savvy

1. The Customer 10
2. A-Team 19
3. The Draft 29
4. Trust 35
5. Need a Vehicle 41
6. Financing 47
7. Act Big 51
8. The Vanishing Organizational Chart 54
9. Engineers at the Helm 57

Part 2 – Technical Acumen

10. Cut It Open 62
11. Vertical Integration 66

12. He Who Tries the Most Things Wins 72
13. Picket Fence Intellectual Property 76
14. In-source 80
15. Effective Meetings 83
16. Electrons Too 86

Part 3 – The Final Act 89

Acknowledgements 94

Foreword

For a couple of years, Derek and I led a large product development project together. He was the lead engineer and I was the product manager. I had always respected Derek from a distance and knew that he was a good engineer. But after working closely together with him for several years, even as his health declined, I came to appreciate just what a unique and talented engineer he really was. He had three special talents rarely possessed by one individual. First, he was an inventor at heart—always the go-to person when we needed a breakthrough idea or creative thinking. Second, he was an exceptional mechanical design engineer—his ability to get the mechanical details right in a cost-effective design set the standard for every engineer to follow. Finally, he had a big-picture business sense that allowed him to grasp quickly the economic or commercial realities of a product concept we were discussing. This powerful combination served Precision Planting well—first as "Engineer #1," as we took to calling Derek, and later in leadership of our research efforts.

After Derek was diagnosed with cancer in 2011 his focus really changed, from being a task-focused doer to being a people-focused teacher. While his physical health was failing, it was a delight to see him grow and develop in this way. In addition to spending time with younger employees, he started working on "his book." After Precision Planting was purchased by Monsanto in the summer of 2012, Derek worked passionately to make sure that the key elements that made Precision successful would be retained to ensure the future success of the company. Those of you who worked with Derek or know him well will hear his voice on every page of this book. Those who didn't will soon learn that Derek had a strong opinion about almost everything—which made discussions with him so enjoyable. He strongly believed that these lessons, many of which run contrary to popular management theories, are vital to the success of any company, but are especially applicable to product-focused startups.

When Derek passed away on July 2, 2014 at the age of 40, we lost not only a husband, father, brother, son, and friend, but also a great co-worker and mentor. Derek's book was still in draft manuscript form on his laptop. But even in its rough state, Derek's convictions and ideas shine through, and we wanted to honor Derek's goal of sharing these lessons from Precision Planting with others. I hope his words can provide comfort for those of us who grieve and inspire all of us to live life with the passion that Derek did.

Doug Sauder

Preface

This book is the culmination of a career as I face the end of my time on earth. In 2011 I was diagnosed with terminal brain cancer. It's not like I was given a certain timespan to live. The doctor gave me some rough estimates but I've already outlived them, and for that I give the credit to the Lord. The realization that life is short has caused me to focus on the important things in life. Part of what I consider important is leaving a written legacy of things I've learned throughout my career. There are other things I've done, including writing letters to my children that they can read as they reach milestones in life. I don't know if I'll be here in person to explain what I've learned to my children. I'm still working as much as I can in spite of many medical appointments. I say this not to seek pity, but to point out that the focus it has brought to my life has been a good thing.

This book is not meant to provide an answer to every problem that a startup company will face over time. It doesn't have solutions to every problem you will ever face. My goal in writing it is to pass along many secrets I've learned over time and through the experiences of my career. I've come to learn that life isn't about hoarding knowledge for ourselves. I certainly can't take it with me. It's about sharing and helping others. It's about lifting up others in life. Life is about teaching others and helping others to be successful in whatever they attempt. For anyone who wants to be successful in business and provide a safe workplace for other people, here are a few lessons to help make the road smoother. I wish you much success on the journey.

Derek Sauder
June 2014

Introduction

When I was ten years old, I started walking beans for my uncle Gregg. When I was in high school and college I worked for my dad, who had his own business drilling wells. After I graduated from college I worked for Caterpillar. I spent three years in the Mining and Construction Equipment Division and two years at the Peoria Proving Grounds. The remaining twelve years I've spent at Precision Planting, both when it was a young company and then in the last couple years after we were bought by a large company.

Many of the secrets I want to share are things I learned from other people. One thing I've learned is that there's power in relationships with others. I've come to see that the people who are different than me in many ways are the ones who can teach me the most. For example, much of what I've learned about business analysis came from an engineer who I'm going to call Bob. The difference in our working styles was stark.

It was frustrating to work with Bob closely at a technical level because of our different styles. When Precision Planting was still a small company with only a few engineers, Bob and I were often at odds. On one particular project that we were working on together, he was more focused on the lab research work and I was doing the production design. He would figure out how to make something work in the lab. Within a few days I would have the design and manufacturability figured out. As soon as I would get the design sent out for quote, Bob would change his mind about what he wanted. You can imagine my frustration as

I dealt with numerous changes. For a few years I viewed this as an insurmountable problem. But over time I began to regard him as a great mentor and co-worker. I learned to appreciate Bob for the perspective he brought to the project. His ability to analyze a project from a financial perspective taught me a lot. Bob also had the ability to think through the decisions that customers would make and how those decisions would influence our products. From Bob, I learned that others have much to teach us, even those with whom at first we disagree.

The time I realized this most clearly was on a flight with Bob coming home from California. We'd gone out there to evaluate a technology that we thought might be useful in manufacturing one of our ideas. After visiting the company we concluded that adopting this new technology would be too risky for Precision Planting. The clincher came when Bob pointed out how expensive and complicated it would be for the farmer to take parts off and install this new device. So we realized that we should kill the project from a commercial perspective alone. Even if we'd been able to solve the technical problems, the product might never have been viable from the customer angle. Bob helped me broaden my perspective beyond that of the engineer's to include the end customer's viewpoint.

The goal of this book is for the reader to implement as many of these lessons as possible. They will help you accomplish more work in less time. The secret to being successful is not to implement each and every element I describe. The more lessons you can implement, the more successful you will be. But if you can only do half, then do that half well. Most of these principles don't require implementing the others in order to bear fruit. There is one lesson, however, that is synergistic: have good employees. This is a prerequisite for many of the other lessons. Good employees are the foundation for many of these principles, and I'll spend a whole chapter discussing this subject. If there's one thing I hope you'll take away from my writing, it's this: Good employees are an invaluable asset and the key to building a good business. If you don't follow this principle in deciding who to hire, I'm not sure that many of the other concepts will help you.

These days, many people are down on U.S.-based manufacturing and opportunities. I hold a much different view. Opportunity abounds locally and the initiative and raw skills can be nourished here. I see much opportunity for innovation at the local level by small business owners and entrepreneurs. I could spend a lot of time discussing our education system and trying to fix that. I could spend time on the nature of our government system. But I've become convinced that the answer to our problems isn't some big program or governmental solution. It's about being in tune with the needs of the younger generation growing up around us, teaching them to think and behave in the right ways. My hope is that by putting the concepts in this book into action, you can be part of the solution to the larger problem of the decline of U.S.-based manufacturing. Many U.S. jobs have been lost in recent years to countries such as China. We have a few choices when we think about responding to this issue. First, we can complain and blame someone else. Second, we can wait around for someone else to fix it—like waiting for the government to come out with a tariff or some other program to help rectify the situation. Third—and this is the answer I like—each business owner can take responsibility for his own company's success. Sure, there are some commodities that are going to be sourced elsewhere. Some changes are inevitable. However, I feel that many of the problems we face as a nation could be fixed if each company had the innovation and strategy to position themselves as a value-added supplier of goods. Offshoring to places like China and India is just a passing fad. As the bean-counters figure out the true costs and the cost of labor in other countries begins to rise, the tide will shift. Stay focused on U.S.-based businesses and you'll find that opportunity abounds.

People thought I was crazy when I left a large company to become the first engineer at a small family-run business named Precision Planting. Those people included my parents, family, and friends. My new employers were my uncle and aunt, Gregg and Cindy Sauder. Many people thought, "Where does Gregg get the money to pay those people?". It was none of their business. He knew what he was doing. It was risky for me, of course. There was no company-provided healthcare at that time. It was a number of years before the company started providing health insurance. A single mistake could've meant the end of the company. One thing I've learned is that in life, risk doesn't always come where you expect it. I've been at Precision Planting for twelve years now. How many times do you think I was worried about my job and the security of the engineers here? Never. Meanwhile the company I left, Caterpillar, has had downturns. I can think of two distinct times when I would have been nervous about losing my job if I'd stayed.

It's funny, when you think about it. On that note, let me tell you another story. I got married during the time I worked at Precision Planting. My wife, Leann, comes from a family where Caterpillar is viewed as the ultimate in security. I know that when we were engaged, some people in her family thought, "I wish he still worked at Caterpillar." The sad thing is, they weren't the only ones, not by any stretch of the imagination. Around our area I would guess half of the people are either employed by Caterpillar or one of their suppliers. So you can imagine how ingrained the idea is, that the pinnacle of success is to work at the "Big Yellow." My father-in-law and brother-in-law work at CAT today. Both have endured short-term layoffs over the last year. So one thing I'd urge you is not to be deceived by a false sense of security in your job.

I'd like to tell you a bit about my relationship with my uncle Gregg. I grew up about an eighth of a mile from his house. He was a farmer and my dad was a well driller. Uncle Gregg was seven years younger than my dad. My brother and I worked for him when we were in grade school and high school. His kids were about ten years younger and down. We formed our relationship walking beans, sorting hogs, building an addition to his house, and riding in the combine. Gregg was familiar with my work ethic and there was no doubt in his mind as to who I was. There was already a lot of good history and trust between us before I left Caterpillar and came to work full-time for him.

Many people wonder why we enjoyed so much success. I don't attribute it to one or the other of us alone. I think Gregg would agree when I say that we had the magic combination of great engineering and great sales. Gregg would've been successful without an engineering group behind him, but the combination is what really built success. You need good details from a technical standpoint, but without good customer sense and marketing it would be almost worthless. Gregg has an extraordinary ability to relate to the American Farmer. There are great speakers who are able to teach their audience while at the same time motivating them to believe that they too can reach the same state of excellence. In this way, Gregg has inspired many farmers who have come to Precision Planting over the years. Each winter and some summers we have a sales conference where we mix motivational speaking with classroom and hands-on instruction. I've heard from a number of attendees who are amazed at the crowd and at how captivating Gregg is as a speaker. This is the mark of a good teacher. You can accurately present the content you're teaching, but if everyone sleeps through the presentation, it's pointless. Gregg has the rare ability to relate to people. His speaking style is phenomenal. The stories he tells have you sitting on the edge of your seat, and he infuses his talks with a sense of humor that makes you feel right at home. He keeps people engaged. That's the first battle in getting anyone to believe what you're telling them. I've come to see this as key to starting a new company and gaining a following. This is why he was able to build Precision Planting into an organization that he could sell twenty years later for a nice return.

Why did I choose this title? Most people think of a serial entrepreneur as a business owner who can't stop starting new businesses. But for me, serial entrepreneurship means constantly creating new and different product lines within the same business. At Precision Planting, we often got into totally new business segments—they were all focused on production agriculture, but they were different in many ways. First, we made planter meters more accurate. Then we got into monitoring systems. After that we were into controlling the planter. Soon we got into the harvesting side of the business. Then we moved into data and mapping operations in the field. The point is that many of the same principles that make a company good at innovating new product lines are also the ones that will guide someone to take on the challenge of starting new businesses.

Throughout this book, you'll frequently hear me refer to "the team." Gregg often says that "it's about getting the right people in the right seats on the bus." I think he may have picked this up from some book he read, but it was a big deal to him, and it was key to our success. No one viewed the company as successful because of one person. Rather, we employed the best people we could and put them into the best positions to match their strengths.

Many books aimed at serial entrepreneurs are about getting funding from venture capitalists and figuring out a way to make hundreds of millions of dollars in a few short years. That does happen once in a while. I'm not going to deny the truth. But that's not what this book is about. This book is about making money over a long period of time, the old-fashioned way. It's about taking care of customers and relating to them honestly. It's about playing a lower-stakes game, both in terms of risk and reward. The rewards are less than with a "swing for the fences" mentality, but so are the risks.

I wasn't born with a great talent for managing or developing people. But I've come to believe that behind every great businessperson there's team of well-positioned employees that make things happen, and so over time I developed an interest in mentoring our younger engineers and helping them grow. This began when my brother joined our team and challenged me to think about our younger engineers. Who was going to mentor them? he asked. Who was going to teach them? I saw the wisdom in this advice, and I began shifting my goal from being a great designer to being a great teacher and coach for a team of great designers.

Part I

Business Savvy

1. The Customer

This seems like the most obvious and well-understood principle among business leaders. It's about being focused on the customer. Any company must know who its customers are and focus on them in order to be successful. There are many ways to stay connected with the customer, and at Precision Planting we had a unique way of doing it. Many companies use focus groups and target interviews to figure out what the customer wants. The amount of time businesses spend on this can be overwhelming, and that's time a small startup doesn't have. Let me propose something that might seem radical. Do none of that. Start by being a customer of your business first. Precision Planting was started by a farmer. His goal was to raise crop yields and help farmers succeed. There was no need to spend huge amounts of time and effort connecting with the customer, because we were the customer. Every day we farmed, our experiences fed right into Precision Planting. These experiences then formed the basis of our business. The problem we were trying to solve was the pain that Gregg had experienced personally as a farmer.

Part of the battle when solving any problem lies in defining it. This is easier to do when you've experienced the problem firsthand. We engineers often spent time riding with Gregg in the tractor cab while he was planting. It isn't hard to see what the problems are when you're that close to the action. Once you can clearly state the problem that must be solved, then you're on the right track. You can learn a lot by listening. Just spend a couple hours with a real user and see what's frustrating him. Planting time was always a time of high pressure, and it's at times like these that you experience the greatest frustrations.

Imagine if you were in the business of building tools for laying a concrete sidewalk faster. You would do a much better job of building those tools if you built sidewalks every day than if you were a farmer. The principles we found to work well for Precision Planting are not unique to farming. They apply to any small business. What I advocate when choosing a business opportunity is to pick something that you inherently understand. You don't want to try to serve people you don't understand well. You want to be in the business selling to people just like yourself. Obviously, if you come up with products and the customer is shaking his head in disbelief, that strategy is not a recipe for success. Being the customer will reduce the errors that come from introducing products that don't make sense for the market.

By the same token, the customer doesn't always know exactly what he needs. There are times when you have to lead him to it. One of our most successful products, DeltaForce, was one that the customer never even asked for. I talk in more detail about this product later, but in brief, the way I determined that there was a need for it was by spending many hours looking at test plot results and Excel files of planting data. A farmer could have seen the same thing by watching a certain screen, spending a lot of time, and being really good at drawing conclusions. The odds were stacked against him, though. What I could do in Excel was far above what the farmer could do in his head, because I had access to special tools available only to engineers. Coming up with product ideas can be either way—it might be something the customer knows he needs, or you might have to educate him of the need for a new product.

There's another reason why product development and sales will be easier when you understand the customer well. When it comes to selling the product, you also need to be able to relate to the customer. It's not just about having the right product. When you have the same concerns and pressures as the consumer, it's easier to relate to him or her. If you're a contractor yourself, you'll have no problem relating to a contractor. If your business is seasonal, you can totally relate to what the potential customer feels like when standing at a trade show in the winter, unsure what the season ahead holds. Your job is to inspire him. If he walks away from your booth with a downbeat attitude, chances are slim that he's going to spend any money. However, if he walks away associating your product or company with business success, then he's a new customer. There's no guaranteeing that he'll buy your product, but I can assure you that this scenario is better than a dejected person walking away.

 I spent many hours riding in tractors and combines with Gregg over the years. From time to time he'd get a call on his cell phone from some farmer he'd met at a show. Obviously, there's a point to minimizing interruptions, but taking those calls was beneficial for two reasons. First, hearing a customer complain about the same things that Gregg was struggling with gave gusto to his opinions about what we should focus on. Second, it was an opportunity to stimulate our market and get people excited. Most successful people gravitate to those with an upbeat attitude.

 The effect of attitudes and outlook are not to be underestimated. Gregg was great at inspiring people to reach for more. We have a choice to sit back and blame others for what isn't right, or we can decide to make things better for ourselves. I'm not going to waste any time discussing the option to be negative. We have to look on the bright side. This is where our products should shine. They're a piece of somebody's solution. If you've got the right attitude and vision, the products you come up with help others and lift them up. This is part of being successful at sales. It's about making an operation better if they buy your product. You're in business with the goal of helping them.

 We had a rule of thumb that we used to gauge whether a product would be successful. First we considered the financial benefit for the customer. If your product has a fifteen-year payback, not many farmers are going to invest in it. However, if it has a half-year payback, then your customer couldn't use poor return as an argument not to buy. Let's take as an example our flagship product, the Keeton Seed Firmer. The Keeton Seed Firmer is a small plastic part that attaches to the planter row unit, ensuring that the planted seed is firmly pressed down into the bottom of the furrow for maximum seed-to-soil contact. It was invented by a farmer in Kentucky, Eugene Keeton. Precision Planting was started in order to market and distribute these seed firmers across the country. When a national magazine evaluated the effectiveness of the seed firmer, they found a five-bushel per acre advantage to using the product. You need one per row to outfit your planter, and a typical planter is used for seventy-five or more acres per row. This worked out to an increased yield for the farmer of 375 bushels per row (75 X 5 = 375). Even at $2.50 per bushel of corn, that was over $900 of extra profit per row. (Corn has been $4-6 per bushel in recent years.) This was the farmer's yield increase for investing in a device that sold for $25 to $30. Based on these numbers, the farmer had no way of arguing that the extra yield wasn't enough. What if it was only one bushel per acre? In that case he would only make $180 per row extra, and should still make the investment. Granted, not all of our products had that level of return. But we always analyzed new products using the same method to gauge their chances of success. It's not about spending days or weeks modeling customer pricing and getting into the decimal points or the sharpness of the pencil. In an hour or less, the question of economics for the farmer can be answered. The seed firmer is a great example of a case where the payback makes sense.

Your calculations should be simple like this. I think calculators have done a big disservice to our working population. I see charts all the time where numbers are reported to multiple decimal points. When SRI—a measure of spacing accuracy for planting seeds—is reported, the numbers usually come out looking something like this: 14.48 vs. 13.78. In reality, we're talking 14 vs. 14, a tie. The reason we always end up struggling to repeat the results of a test is that we've implied and assumed more accuracy in our measurements than is actually possible in the experiment. Tools like calculators and Excel have caused this in part.

When co-workers in meetings are still diving for their calculators, I've already moved on to the next segment of the problem, having worked out a close-enough answer in my head. I'm convinced that many problems in financial or technical analysis are due to carrying around way more decimal points than necessary. If we just estimate the number of corn acres per grower to 10 acres/row of accuracy, it's silly to figure his cost to pennies per row. Tens of dollars per row is sufficient for most products, while on some products the nearest hundred dollars is sufficient.

I had a college professor who once said, "If you can't do the calculation on the back of an envelope, it's not worth doing." He was mostly right. Finite Element Analysis is one area that can't be done without decimal points. However, I would maintain that analysis is more often inaccurate because of assumptions and boundary conditions rather than because of the precision of the calculations. There's a time and place for highly precise models or calculations, but getting to the root cause properly is usually the issue. I discuss this issue in more depth in Part II, Chapter 1: "Cut It Open."

The second criterion that we used to gauge the likely success of a product was ease of use. You need to make your new product easier to use than the one the customer is already employing. If he sees that your product makes his life easier, you've got a customer. Let me talk a little about a product that really made Precision Planting a house name. We developed a kit for seed meters that increased their accuracy in a revolutionary way, called eSet. It wasn't that expensive, but it was pricier than the Keeton Seed Firmer. The "meter" is the part of the planter that plants a single seed at a time out of a hopper that is filled with a whole bag of seeds. eSet is incredibly easy to use. For each crop, there's only one degree of freedom to attaining the desired performance. This is obtained by adjusting the vacuum level on the planter, which can be adjusted easily by turning a knob in the cab. And it's not that sensitive to the correct level, so it's really easy to use. Contrast that to most of our competitors who have at least two things you can tweak to get optimal performance. They have a meter where you can adjust the vacuum level or adjust things mechanically on each row. And the two are interrelated such that there are multiple near-optimum solutions. The result is that you might get acceptable performance in the shop on a narrow operating condition but the solution is not robust to field conditions.

In order to achieve this ease of use, we did give up some flexibility when it came to using the seed meter for different crops. For example, in order to switch to specialty crops like edible beans and sugar beets, you needed to switch a part called the singulator. For 95% of corn growers, we delivered a system in which they didn't have to make multiple adjustments to achieve acceptable performance. My brother called this approach "BDS"—brain-dead simple. The competition had an "easy" adjustment to accomplish this function. Sure, it was easy to adjust on a test stand in the shop but not as easy on the planter. You had to physically go to every row. In addition, it's hard to know what the correct setting should be. It could change for every different field of the same crop.

Another way of thinking about this issue is by asking the question, "What causes stress for the operator?" Sure, some people don't care about the job they do. However, let's assume we're talking about a conscientious worker or a farmer who cares a lot about doing a good job of planting corn. He could wonder all day, "Should I adjust my vacuum level up or down by one inch of water?" This is an easy adjustment to make on newer tractors. You just turn a knob in the cab. The ease of adjusting the vacuum level is only part of the issue. Because eSet didn't require the farmer to be that accurate, he could set the vacuum level and forget about it. It was one more thing he didn't have to worry about. Strive to eliminate decisions that an operator must think about throughout his day—those decisions are a source of stress.

Another useful criterion we discovered was this: The performance should be better than the status quo. Making a product better is the part most engineers have no problem with.

But sadly, many engineers can't see the first two principles and thus work forever developing a technically superior product that few people will buy. They fail to realize that as long as it makes the customer money and is easy to use, the answer is the same. They'll buy the product.

I had a coworker in my first job who used the phrase "it's time to shoot the engineer." At the time I just thought it was funny, but later in my career I saw the truth in what he said. We were working on a hydraulic valve that controlled the lowering of the body (or bed) on a quarry truck. This resulted in a feature called "snubbing," which created a softer landing and thus less shock to the operator. We could have tweaked this feature for a long time but the point was that we'd already made a big difference in functionality. Later on I'd work with engineers who were never satisfied with their work and kept tweaking or worse yet, starting from scratch on a design. But the tiny extra improvement you get from this kind of obsessive fiddling doesn't make much difference to the customer.

You won't succeed with a grossly inferior product, but the most successful product in the market doesn't need to be the absolute best product from a technical standpoint. For the customer, the top three products on the market might be interchangeable, performance-wise. They'll be the same technically, even though there might be slight differences in performance. He may believe for one reason or another that the return is greater for product X or that it is simpler to order, install, or operate. As a product developer, one must keep all these aspects in mind and not get overly focused on one aspect. The customer doesn't know what you could have delivered a couple years later at three times the cost. You have to be wise about how much effort and time to put into making the performance beat the competition.

The last criterion is that the product has to provide you enough profit to stay in business and be rewarded for the risk you took. If you can meet all four criteria I've described above, it doesn't really matter how sophisticated your analysis or planning is, the profits will come. We fueled a lot of research by selling $10-$30 products that made the customer money, were easy to understand and use, and cost us a few dollars to make. Sure, there are costs other than raw production costs—don't think I'm forgetting about those. I mean marketing, selling, and overhead type of costs.

The real reason that being a customer pays off is organizational efficiency and rapid development. Here's a simple example. You're working on a mechanical detail: putting a screw in place. You know that farmers are in the dirt, and a Phillips screwdriver is a common tool. Therefore, you keep the size and accessibility larger than necessary, even though your little desk jockey fingers could easily manipulate a smaller screw. The farmer will be glad you thought of him when he drops it in the dirt. He might not be so happy if it's a small screw with a Torx head that he might not have a screwdriver for, or else the screwdrivers back in his shop. These kinds of decisions come up all the time. The more an engineer understands the customer, the quicker and better these decisions get made. The alternative would be a design review, or a meeting, or worse yet, a focus group. Lots of time can slip past as you schedule and host these types of meetings with customers. Better to do the design right the first time. This isn't to say that you'll never need customer feedback, but it's clunky and expensive to obtain it in this manner.

I'll conclude this by talking a bit about large Original Equipment Manufacturers (OEMs). It doesn't matter which one you choose, as they're all pretty much the same. They have a certain market share in the industry. Oddly enough, the strength of the local dealerships is the most important factor in who has what market share. (I'm referring specifically to the agricultural industry.) These large corporations are slow to make changes. They don't want to screw up the things they think they have going for them, though they might not be right about what those things are. They just build what the customer wants. I've seen companies with very detailed lists of what the farmer wants. These are combinations of what he truly needs and what he thinks he wants because "that's the way Grandpa did it."

Often the customer knows less about what he wants than people who've studied the data and know a planter inside and out. There are customer features that can be important, but if you're a customer yourself and spend time talking to others, you'll know what those are and design those features in. In many industries, the small startup has nothing if it doesn't take on risk. Sometimes the big company may make a big bet and lose the farm, but most of the time the small startup does the innovation and the big company plays catch-up. Having a personality that is at least part visionary is a requirement for being a successful entrepreneur. To successfully innovate rather than just copy, you have to lead the market in new directions. This is true in consumer devices as well as agricultural equipment. Products like the smart phone were truly innovations. Many products, if we stop and look back, have been the same way.

What was unique about Precision Planting? Gregg was first and foremost a farmer. He could see things from a farmer's perspective right away. He drilled that into our heads. Many of us had some connection to and interest in farming. Gregg's farming operation was housed in the same building as the engineering team for many years. We could ride in the planter or combine with him. We understood the needs of the industry. And we could anticipate the customer's needs.

We've started to see after twenty years in the agricultural industry that big companies are starting to innovate. However, we're still much faster and can outrun them. We just can't stop or they'll catch up with us. This is why speed to market is an issue I emphasize again and again in this book.

2. A-Team

What do we mean when we say A team, or All-Stars? It's the quality of all the members on the team. At the core, a lot of personnel issues come down to whether you believe employees are a liability or an asset. Good managers and good companies view them as assets. Once again, I'm speaking about small companies in high-margin, innovative types of business. I'm not talking about a production worker doing some kind of manual labor in a business that produces a commodity. If the example is picking heads of lettuce and you need to hire twenty-five more workers to pick lettuce because your efficiencies are decreasing, then they should be looked at as liabilities. However, if it's more engineers to build better tools for the lettuce pickers to use, thus increasing their job safety or output, those are assets. And if you only have enough work to justify the extra employee for a year, hire him anyway. If your employees are good and innovative people, by the time they get done with the first project, they'll have seen two, three or four other ideas that need to be investigated. Good people turned loose will just keep churning out good stuff.

It's tempting to view engineers as vending machine goodies. You may think, "I need two designers for a couple months and then a tester or two for another month." So you hire a couple contract engineers in a hurry who are average or below in their speed, knowledge, and so forth. As a result your project takes longer than you expected, and you end up using below-average workers for a long time. Whereas if you just hired someone good early on, you'd be done already and have moved on to the next opportunity.

I say this first as a reminder to myself. This hiring concept is hard to stick to after you have thirty-plus engineers on board. Maybe it's because we're owned by a large company now. Maybe we've exhausted the labor pool, which is not an insignificant issue in some locations. Maybe it's the result of decisions forced upon us. It could be a combination of all of these factors. Let me illustrate how it goes now. We realize that a project has a shortcoming that can be solved by adding another person. We beg for requisitions, which is sometimes a long process. Then we think we've exhausted the pool of good talent. We need someone fast, so we hire a contractor we wouldn't hire as a full-time employee because we need someone quick. Pretty soon it's been a few years, and that person's still working in the office. We should've hired a good person, but they weren't available. Contrast that with hiring a good person when he comes along, even though we don't need him full-time by the book. Then, when a need comes up, he's there already. Perish the thought! If we planned more realistically, we might not need him in a panic. I'm not speaking of times when we've hired good people as contract employees because that was the only option we had. Regardless, this is an area where you need to think long-term. If you hire in a panic and get sub-par talent, in a few years you'll have a group of sub-par people.

There have been a few exceptions to this rule, where we found that contract employees were really good. But more often than not, the result is that we wish we'd gotten rid of them faster. It's often the case that within a few weeks you can tell what kind of employee a new hire will be. Sometimes an employee takes a while to develop, but that's not normally the case. My conclusion over the years has been that problems are best dealt with quickly, and delaying doesn't do any favors for either side.

I'm not saying that every decision and policy made at Precision Planting over the years was the right one or the best one possible. We've made messes out of a few situations that could've been handled better. However, the general atmosphere at our company was that employees were valued, and we respected what each person contributed to the team. If there was a time when someone was underpaid, it wasn't because we felt that the way to make the company successful was to save a few thousand dollars on payroll. It was just inattention, neglect of detail, or maybe some naivete as to what the market was paying. In the long term, an organization can only be successful if they reward people financially as well as position them in line with their talents. I'm not talking about pay increases to underperforming employees. I'm talking about rewarding good people and laying out a plan where they can continue to receive increases in compensation as they gain more experience and take on more responsibility.

You have to start with valuing your employees and believing, deep down, that they have the power to make you and your company great to do business with. If you've ever owned your own business, you probably understand this already. Gregg would often say that it was great employees who made Precision great. Why does it really matter if you have good employees? I'll try to answer that question in the next six paragraphs.

Reason #1: Less management and quick results. When a manager communicates with an average employee, he has to explain the big picture and then has to stay involved in a number of ways. He has to make more decisions for the average employee. An engineer who is sharp and understands the customers and all factors of the project will make these decisions quickly as he goes. He'll keep the timeline in mind when making design decisions, both as it relates to design effort, tooling time, and cost. The time spent giving an average engineer ideas, keeping an eye on every detail of his timeline, and watching the product cost is all wasted, both on the part of the manager and the employee. A good engineer just does this stuff naturally. And success comes more quickly to him. It's partly because his ideas are better and partly because he has better working methods. I'm talking primarily about design time here, because time is money.

This was particularly true at Precision Planting because of the seasonality of our work. Most of our products are focused on corn planting in the United States. This happens over the course of about two months, in April and May. If we don't have a new product shipped to the customer in time for him to install it a few weeks before planting, he waits till next year. So for us, if we miss by a month, we have to wait another year. The farmer only plants corn once per year. Obviously there are some exceptions with other crops and other regions, but timing is everything.

Reason #2: A small, highly efficient team can get more done than a big cumbersome team. A major impetus for keeping small teams of highly competent people is communication. This becomes particularly apparent in formal scheduled meetings. I'm going to assume that you have a capable manager directing any meetings so they stay on schedule. But even with that, everyone takes their time speaking their mind. It's tough to shut people out. The more people who have a say, the more time it will take to work something out. Then there's the informal stuff. You run over to an employee's desk to ask a project-related question but get sucked into a discussion about how to fix his flooring around the kitchen sink. And then you find out it wasn't employee A that you needed to talk to but rather employee B. You can't eliminate all wasted time and recreational discussion in an organization, but my point is that this amount of time becomes larger as the team size grows. For this reason, one or two people sitting right next to each other, working on a project together, can get a lot done.

Reason #3: Good employees are quick to help each other. So far I've focused a lot on the productivity and cost side of the equation. But there's another reason to hire top talent. I had a couple of employees who came from the same large company thank me for the environment we had at Precision. What they noticed was that everyone they worked around was top talent. There was no one "doing time" until retirement. Everyone was pulling together for the common good. Because no one was perceived as a "freeloader," everyone was willing to help each other. They placed a high degree of trust in one another, and weren't afraid of being let down by their co-workers. Another important component, which I'll touch on later, is that you have to maintain an environment that is competitive but not one in which employees see each other as threats. But this starts with employees having a high regard for each other, and that can only happen when you are recruiting good talent for your team. An engineer is more than a number, and many HR departments miss this point when setting recruiting goals. Rather than focusing on how many engineers you have working on a project, you should focus on how many good ones you have.

Reason #4: More flexibility. When your company is evaluating a future project, having a team of all-stars is a dream come true. If everyone can only do a certain part of the job, you'll end up needing John first, then Bill, then Dean, then John again. Contrast this with an organization where everyone is good. You can use Bill, Dean, John or whoever, depending on who's available for the duration of the project. I'm not talking about your programmers being good mechanical engineers. I'm talking about a mechanical engineer being good at cost estimation, figuring out manufacturing, making prints, building Pro/E models, putting the design together, testing it, and working with customers in the field. I realize not everyone will be that good, but the more people you have like that, the easier it is to staff and manage projects.

This is really important for smaller companies. Our second engineer could do both of two important tasks: he had done a fair amount of instrumentation and programming in college, and he could also design mechanical things. We put this knowledge to use in a couple ways. In the early days, we needed the flexibility to handle multiple types of projects because we didn't have many people. But as we grew, it was still valuable to have an engineer who could do both the electrical and mechanical side of a project. We often gave him projects that needed both and let the purely mechanical engineers work on purely mechanical projects.

The same can be said for research versus production design. I had skills in both areas, and it paid off especially well on early projects. For example, on eSet, I wasn't the only guy on the research side. I focused primarily on production. But I still spent countless hours in the lab. I spent enough time that I understood the intricacies well enough to get the production design correct.

Reason #5: Better relationships with your customers and suppliers. It doesn't take much thinking to figure this one out. I called the phone company a few months back and got a person on the line who didn't know much about customer service. She'd been told to sell more expensive plans. When she asked me if she could search for a different plan that fit me better, I said, "If it costs less." She couldn't understand that, and persisted in trying to sell me a more expensive plan for fewer minutes. I told her I didn't have time and hung up. Then I went into one of their stores and was attended to by someone who honestly wasn't sharp enough to run the computer. She had to ask for help with every question I had. Needless to say, I didn't have a very high opinion of that company. Two of the three people I dealt with were working way above their potential. So I viewed them as mostly incompetent people working for an overpaid company. This matters a great deal, unless your employees have no chance of interfacing with a customer or supplier. That might be true in a big company, but it's certainly not true in a company with ten or fifty employees.

We put a high priority on taking good care of our suppliers as well. Good employees are part of this. You earn respect if you're logical and thoughtful. There are a couple things that these contract suppliers think are valuable. The first is timeliness in paying bills. I can't say we were never late, but in general bills were always paid within thirty days. By contrast, the larger companies were cool with stretching payments out to ninety days. A couple of our employees came from the automotive purchasing world and knew that area well. In that business, quoting a new part involved many political games such as "cost downs" over time, which didn't help the timelines any.

Remember that doing a good job but also moving quickly is an important but often overlooked part of any business.

Whether interfacing with customers or suppliers, having competent employees is key. We all know that the requests of the people we sell to must make sense. It doesn't matter if this is working with tolerances and dimensions in part development, or trying experiments, or what you are doing together. Both parties feel better when there is competence on both sides of the table.

I have a theory I like to call the "black box theory." It's a concept I learned in college. Let's say you want to analyze the power going into a system consisting of a tractor and an implement. You draw a box around the tractor and the implement and think about the forces acting upon it. You look at the whole system, not just little pieces. In our case, the whole system was the supplier, us, and the customer. In this case we're just thinking about the supplier. If we draw a black box around them and us, we can answer many questions that come up. For example, if we can brush a hole with graphite better than the supplier can at lower cost, we might as well do it ourselves. When it comes to thinking about costs, we don't want to be too hard on them. We need to be smart about it, and realize what drives cost through the production process, then eliminate it, rather than expecting the supplier to do it on their own dime and lose money. In the long term, that would only cost us money and time because they would end up quitting on us, and we'd have to re-source at a higher cost. The best solution is to look out for each other's interests and work together. I'm convinced that higher-caliber employees think this way much easier than average employees do.

Reason #6: Rewarding employees well doesn't really cost that much. I've thought about how best to illustrate this and don't see any way other than some hypothetical figures. There are also a few realities that you have to accept first. The first is productivity. Some managers and accountants think that engineers are just a number and they're all equal. Anyone who has actually managed people and been realistic about it knows that it takes different amounts of time for different people to accomplish the same task. There was a point where we had a CFO who'd come from a different type of business, one where employees were regarded in many ways as a commodity. He wanted more projects done in a given year. He couldn't understand why we couldn't just hire five more mechanical engineers and get the job done. A couple things were going on here. First off, we didn't have any engineers waiting in our network, so we didn't really have people available to hire. Secondly, we didn't have the management available to train new hires. A new engineer needs at least a little guidance. It's different than someone whose job is basically the same industry-wide, regardless of which company they work for. We in R&D held to our belief that engineers are unique, having their own abilities and talents. Looking back, I wouldn't change that decision.

Let's get back to our analogy. Imagine that we have a project of a size that requires four excellent engineers or six good ones. Right away we see the direct labor cost of four versus six employees. Anyone who has worked in any field of research or development or CAD drawing, print creation, etc. will agree that there can be a 50% difference in productivity. First, let's look at the salary side of the equation. Suppose an average engineer makes around $80,000 doing this sort of work. If I have a total budget of $480,000 to pay engineers' salaries, I could afford to hire four excellent engineers at $120,000 a year instead of six good ones at $80,000. In the marketplace, this is huge. "Overpaying" an engineer by $40,000 will surely attract top talent. And we haven't even begun to capture all the costs associated with having only so-so talent. It might take 40% of a manager's time to manage four excellent engineers, while managing six less effective employees might take 70% of his time. That's another 30% of a $100,000 salary. Now I can afford to give the four excellent engineers $127,500 instead of $80,000.

As I continue this explanation, it becomes harder to quantify the costs and benefits. So I'm going to stop calculating, figuring that if at this point the numbers haven't convinced you, nothing will. And then there are the costs associated with a desk or shop space, all the overhead related to having additional employees, including benefits, for example. Things like profit sharing and 401k match do scale with salary, but many of the costs, such as insurance, have nothing to do with salary. So it's cheaper to pay fewer employees to do a job.

Lest we get the wrong attitude, it's not all about the money. There are many other factors that relate to job happiness more than just raw salary: lack of bureaucracy, results that employees can see from their work, good relationships with coworkers and bosses, good working hours and conditions, and so forth. There were times when we let prospective candidates go over money. We knew we were offering to compensate them well, but we sensed that their happiness was more about the money than about job satisfaction. We wanted someone who was coming because of our organization and its characteristics more than just the money.

The point I'm trying to make here is that employees are not a liability. A good employee is every bit worth the salary. You won't get ahead by trying to nickel-and-dime on salaries. And just to remind you, I'm coming from the background of a company where we sold items that resulted in hundreds of thousands or maybe a million dollars of net margin the first year alone. We weren't even close to the point where engineers were a bad return. But even if you're manufacturing something and you have just one or two engineers in a support role, it's hard to justify low salaries. Maybe you need "half" an engineer, and you hire one poor one instead of one good or great one. If you're in that position, I'm not really writing to you. But if you want to develop many new products quickly, it's worth your while to consider these questions.

I'm not sure I even realized what a great team we'd built. I knew we had good engineers on the team and was thankful for their good attitudes. It was rare that we had to deal with a skeptic or someone who didn't fit in. There were a couple times when we had people like that, and they moved on to other opportunities. One thing I did when I was able was to take the guys out to lunch. I have trouble eating now, so I haven't been able to do this as much. I tried to make a point of picking someone once a week and taking them to lunch for a couple hours. It was good for a several reasons. First, it made the engineers feel connected to the larger picture. They could share frustrations, they could ask me anything. It's amazing how far it goes toward building good relations with employees to just set aside time to talk. I realized what a great team we had when one of the engineers mentioned this to me. He said that there was never someone looking over your shoulder on a project. He had a high degree of trust in all his co-workers and knew anyone would help him. He was amazed by the skill level of the people he worked with. He'd come from Caterpillar and had experienced some of the cut-throat attitudes and free-loading spirit that exist in other companies. This isn't rocket science. Just spend time with your employees and they'll feel better about their job, and you'll be more in touch with their needs.

3. The Draft

I'd like to convince you of a different way of hiring top talent. Let's start with the normal way a position is filled. After I graduated from college, I had only three companies seriously interested in hiring me. The first was a large multinational, and they were pretty crafty in their interviewing. They obviously had their game figured out. I didn't realize it until I was on the plant trip for the second company, when I understood the game a little better. They interviewed me once on campus, then once or twice over the phone. Then they invited me out to their headquarters to meet with their managers and see their labs. In many of the interviews, I was asked the same questions over and over again. They were worthwhile questions, helping my potential employer figure out who I was and how I approached problems. But eventually I figured out that the main thing they were trying to assess was how consistent I was. They wanted to see the same strong answer, rather than multiple answers. I found out later that this is called the STAR method. It's better than nothing, for sure. But I never saw a process like this at Precision.

In the early days, Gregg was present at all of our job interviews. At first it struck me as weird. He rarely asked for a resume. He wouldn't have known what to do with one if he saw it. Mostly he just cared about one thing, and if that one thing was missing, he'd have a hard time getting excited about a candidate. He wanted to see how passionate and eager a person became during the interview. If they started throwing out design ideas, that was a good sign. If they got excited about the company, that was a good sign. We were looking for emotional fit. When he interviewed me (which he did twice) it wasn't really an interview but a sales session. Gregg had been familiar with my character and work ethic since I was a young boy. When I was ten years old I'd walked beans for him and Grandpa, so he knew I could work. I'd helped build his house, work with his pigs, build grain systems, give whatever extra help he needed around the farm. He wasn't checking me out. He was trying to convince me to leave a "stable" job and come to a startup company. (I was about the twelfth employee in the company when I came on board.) People thought I was nuts. They couldn't figure out why I'd leave a large company where I had it made. They just didn't see the spark and the vision that Gregg had lit inside of me. By the way, that big company is now entering a second phase of dealing out permanent layoffs. By contrast, we've never been in layoff mode, but have added engineers every year. So much for what we think of as a "safe" job.

Not every candidate we hired had a family connection. But it was rare that we were hiring total strangers. Usually someone inside the company had recommended the person because they knew them and had likely worked with them at some point. So a lot of the time that in an average interview would be used to assess character, we skipped in order to focus on whether the candidate caught the vision of what we were doing. And it's amazing, in an interview you can tell pretty easily whether someone catches your vision or not. There's a fire that lights up the eyes of someone who catches and shares your passion.

As the company got bigger, Gregg stopped participating in all the interviews. And we started reaching out to people we were a little less connected to. But we still focused on our network of contacts and geared our interviews primarily toward making sure that the applicants were excited and passionate.

When we were a small company, the scope of the job was hardly an issue at all. We had so few people that everyone knew that the scope of the job was wide open. It was kind of funny; we made it up to the last couple years without even having a written job description. With the people we tried to hire, it wasn't much of an issue. If we saw that they had a broad range of skills, we knew we'd put them to use. As we got larger, we had a number of roles where were we could specifically define the scope of what we needed them to do. It helped us ensure that we were getting the right guy for the right job.

My conclusion to all this is that the smaller your organization is, the less structure you want, and less you want written out. Your people need to be sharp and flexible. As you get larger, your skill sets can get more specific. But don't be afraid to have things organized a bit loosely. Good people will do more for innovation in your company than you can imagine.

Obviously things have changed a little as we've gotten larger—say, in the 15-40 engineer size range. We've become more focused on narrow job descriptions. And we're focusing less on their potential than on the question, "Can they do this job?"

One thing we did that might seem weird was administering aptitude tests to potential applicants. A friend of mine tipped me off to this technique, and it has worked well over the years. Our families had known each other since we were little kids in school. His family ran a manufacturing business, and at the time I went to Precision he was the engineering manager of his family business. He had roughly thirty guys working for him. He was like us in that he hired local kids whose families he knew and whose work ethics he was familiar with. He offered them internships so he could observe their workmanship. And he gave them a few standardized tests to place where their aptitude was. One of the tests was a mechanical aptitude test. He said he'd never seen a case where someone with poor mechanical aptitude could be a good engineer. He did a personality test as well, and could pretty much peg how someone would interact with others. We didn't find the personality test as helpful. Maybe we weren't administering the test correctly and using the results well. It was just harder to know what to do with the results. We avoided a few mistakes through the mechanical aptitude testing. Someone might interview well, but if they had poor mechanical aptitude, we wouldn't offer them the job. Many times the test results and the interview results would go hand in hand, but not always.

Another test I gave many times was a personnel test to assess an applicant's ability to learn. This came in really handy with guys who were looking for internships. I didn't have much work experience to go on. But I found that if someone could learn quickly, it didn't matter what they knew. And most times I'd see that the people who were slow learners didn't have as much knowledge as I needed. So I stuck to fast learners when I was hiring. This really paid off. I know most people find test results confusing and are unsure of how to use them. But your emotions can lie to you, so this helps you form a better picture of a candidate.

I regret that we didn't make better use of interns in our early years. When we had about five full-timers in our department, a kid whose family was one of our customers stopped by a farm show and asked Gregg if he could work at Precision while he went through engineering school. Gregg told me a little about him and suggested that I get together with him. I did, and I remember that he didn't know much about what he wanted to do. He was just starting junior college, so it wasn't like he had a career path nailed down. He wanted to farm but was allergic to dust, and he knew it wasn't feasible for him to plan on farming with his family. So we took him on as an intern when he was a freshman or sophomore in college.

Now my philosophy towards teaching is that you throw someone into the mess and if they learn what to do by teaching themselves, they will be good. Or if you show them once and they get it, it's not too bad either. This was definitely the case with most of our interns. They typically got it and contributed right from the start. I remember when the intern I mentioned above challenged me on something I had taught him. He was right and I knew then that we had someone on our hands who could learn quickly and think for himself. We had a couple interns who weren't that great. But it was a good way to see who someone was without wasting a lot of money.

And then there was the side benefit of recruiting for full-time employment. It was easier to snag someone if they'd worked for us in college than if they hadn't. Looking back, we should have done more of this and been a little more strategic about it. We could have filled more of our open slots with less work if we'd utilized this more as a recruiting tool. I know we wouldn't have gotten the intern I described above if he hadn't seen how we worked and been able to contribute so much even while in college. Now we're doing a better job of making sure one or two of our interns graduate every May. We'll see if we're positioned well over the next few years, but we're better off than we were years ago.

I don't know if you've picked up on this yet or not, but I don't think that we in R&D ever hired someone who was currently unemployed. We'd usually call someone up out of the blue and try to sell them on working for our company. Once in a while we'd find someone who was receptive because they were tired of the bureaucracy in a large organization. Usually we'd find someone who was willing to meet with us but was happy where they were at currently. And they'd make great employees. Usually the unemployed are unemployed for a reason, so you have to be careful. I'm not talking about new college grads; of course they're unemployed.

Shared values are also important. We're a pretty homogeneous group of people, and we wouldn't have the camaraderie we do today if that weren't the case. We've discussed trying to cast our net a little wider, but there's something about everyone sharing the same values that really makes our company a special place to work. Our organization is primarily made up of farm kids. Many have had a Christian upbringing. We're almost entirely men. None of these factors are mandatory in any sense, and there are a number of exceptions. We'd much rather hire a Midwestern farm kid than an East Coast city kid. It's not that we're prejudiced about their abilities. It's for a couple other reasons. A Midwestern farm kid will identify with and understand the customer much more quickly. He'll also be content to remain in the area and work for us for a longer period of time. We don't benefit by hiring someone who's just passing through for a couple years. I know this is an area that many companies struggle with. But in my assessment, shared values are an important reason why our team has gelled and worked together so well.

4. Trust

I've seen a couple ways of managing a business. One is based on trust. The other is based on fear. Let me work in the organization running on trust any day. I can think of lots of examples on this subject. Gregg placed an amazing amount of trust in his people. In general he had learned what to expect from whom. He knew who he could trust and who he couldn't. I'm talking to a certain degree about employees, but mostly just people in the community. It wasn't that he had a blind trust in everyone. It was something he learned from experience.

Contrast this with the experiences we've had since being acquired by a large company. Large companies tend to run businesses based on the assumption that process and controls are what should be trusted, rather than individuals. There's no process by which a person earns trust and is then trusted.

Let's start by looking at just the financial side of the equation. In the days PP was an independent company, we made our financial decisions in some surprising ways. We did things to save the company money. In general, we spent money like it was our own. We were careful when we made an engineering change to a tool, doing this only when the cost to the company was justified. We made sure we understood everything about a change we were considering, so that we could do it efficiently from a cost standpoint. I'm sure that if you found some way to measure what we got done with the money spent, we'd turn out to be pretty efficient overall.

Travel is just one example of this concept. Perhaps it's the one where we can see the difference most clearly. For example, before we were acquired, we were allowed to use whatever means were honest to book a motel room. There was no corporate maximum per-night rate policy. There was no corporate method for booking a room. Now we're part of a large corporation. We have a $150 maximum per night for hotel stays, and a corporate system we must use that supposedly gets us a discount. So get this. Last year, while we were still an independent company, I went to the Holiday Inn where we did a lot of business and asked for a discounted business rate since we would have multiple engineers there for several months. We paid something like $95 per night. This year, we are booking the exact same motel through the corporate system. We are paying $140 per night. Maybe there's been a little inflation in Texas, but almost 50% increase in one year? And get a load of this: Traveling and checking in together at this same motel are one of our contract employees and one of our full-time employees. Don't quote me on the exact numbers, but the contractor is paying about $40 less a night than we are. All because he booked his stay on his own online. This illustrates a couple things. First, it makes you wonder what's going on with the corporate travel people and what they've fallen for. Second, it's tough to keep an attitude of "costs matter" when you see that the corporate travel budget is about something other than keeping costs down.

Meals are another example. In the past we didn't have to submit any receipts, we were just allotted $30 per day. It might not work out every day, but over a trip, this was definitely fair. And it saved a lot of time. Now we're limited to $50 per meal, but we have to have an itemized receipt. So the guys go into a diner in Texas and spend $8. They've never heard of an itemized receipt in a remote area like this, and they have no way to give us one. So the engineer ends up wasting time asking for one, and has to do some funny business on his expense report over an $8 meal. How ridiculous. It sends employees the message that their time at work isn't to be spent on productive activities, but rather monkey business, because their employer does not trust them.

I was getting ready for a trip on which my wife wanted to go along, and we didn't want to fly for health reasons. I also knew we would both drive, and it was against company policy to have a non-employee drive a rental car. So instead of renting, I turned in partial mileage for our own vehicle that would about equal the cost of renting a car and buying gas for it. It was less than the IRS allows but covered our expenses and didn't cost the company extra. The expense report was approved and paid, so I thought everything was fine. Then I got an audit email saying that they need a record of mileage for the three-day trip broken down by day. I know that audits are a way of teaching employees the rules. But making me waste fifteen minutes filling out another form is just another example of a situation in which results don't matter, of the kind of silliness that happens when you don't trust your employees.

And these attitudes will start to affect every decision we make. I've seen it happen already. It's not our money. There's plenty of it. It comes from some big company in the sky. You can be sure in the future I will fill out the form and turn in all the miles. This is the attitude these policies build. Not by intention and goal, but that's what happens.

So that's the financial side of why you want employees you can trust. But there are reasons other than financial ones to run a business this way. One is the amount of time you spend double-checking decisions and assumptions. I learned early on how to read Gregg, and developed a sort of gut feel for whether he would go for something or not. It was like any business in that a certain amount of time needed to be spent explaining what we were doing and getting Gregg's feedback on certain features. I remember only one time in eleven years when Gregg questioned something we were going to do financially. One of the other engineers had made a recommendation that we spend $75,000 on a tool for research and development. It would allow us to replay field conditions on row units and was really necessary to get to the bottom of some problems we were having in the field. I remember distinctly the call from Gregg, and where I was when I got it. He just asked if I was sure we needed to spend this much money, and I assured him I didn't see any other way, and that was the end of it. That probably doesn't sound like a lot of money to you, but that was early on and money didn't come easy. The amazing thing is, that's the only time I can remember when anyone questioned the money I was spending. Can you imagine the amount of time we saved not having to write up requisitions, not having to send approvals around? Because we trusted each other, we could just innovate at high speed and not be looking over our shoulders or stuck in bureaucracy.

Another reason to trust employees is innovation itself. Employees who enjoy liberty and freedoms will innovate more. Think about it this way. If all the decisions are made at the top and are handed down through several layers of managers, it's hard to feel much ownership and responsibility. What happens is you develop an attitude of, "Tell me what to do and I'll do it," rather than the attitude we had, which was, "Tell me the problem and I'll fix it."

For years Gregg was convinced that there must be a better way to adjust row cleaners. (A row cleaner is an attachment to the planter row unit that uses toothed wheels to move old corn stalks or other residue away from the area where the new seed will be planted.) On the model that we liked, a backup nut and half-inch bolt had to be adjusted in order to "set" them. This involved using a couple wrenches and trying to avoid skinning your knuckles. There are many sharp points on row cleaners and avoiding them is not easy. Often we complained to each other about how hard this was to do. This was a problem just waiting for a solution from R&D. And we just stumbled into one, because—you can trace this theme through to other chapters as well—we were also the customer. It was Memorial Day weekend, and Gregg had a small field of silage corn to plant. His other planter was too big to mess with in order to plant this little field, so he asked me to take R&D's twelve-row planter over and plant it. We had just put a plot in on the previous Friday and the soil conditions in that field were very firm. This field by contrast was the loosest I had ever seen. It was in a river bottom, so the soil was sandy in nature. And if I remember correctly it had been plowed, so it was very loose. We spent an hour trying to adjust all the row cleaners to get things right. And then it hit me. The bolts were the wrong solution in the first place. The solution was a pneumatic cylinder so the row cleaner could float up and down. With the air pressure rapidly adjustable, you could adjust all rows at one moment's time from the cab. We went from a brainwave on Memorial Day weekend to a product called CleanSweep, which sold thousands of rows the next spring. I don't normally suggest moving that quickly, but the nature of the design and parts we were using did not require development. This product turned out to be a huge success for the company. It didn't come by bureaucracy. It came because the owner trusted an employee and the innovation just happened.

Let's talk a little about living by fear. Being acquired by a large company has given us ample opportunities to witness this mindset. This company has a policy that if any risk or problem can be imagined, then paying any amount of money to mitigate that risk is worth it. Talk about bringing an organization to a grinding halt out of fear that something bad might happen. I'm not talking about obvious safety polices with personal protective equipment and such. That doesn't cost much to put in place, and is obviously one of the higher-incidence accidents that can be avoided. For every problem there's a risk of it happening and a cost to implementing a solution. I know there will be many out there who don't agree with me, but in my mind, there's a happy medium. If the cost to implement a solution is low, or the risk of a problem happening is high, then you fix it. But paying high costs to avoid low risks is a drag on the business. Doing so sends the message to employees that common sense shouldn't be used. It tells employees to worry more about procedures than getting work done. There's a middle ground here. You don't want to be reckless, or employees will think that you don't value their lives and safety, which is a bad position to be in. I used to work in a town that was home to a large employer with a reputation for having lots of bad accidents. It wasn't good for the family members or friends of employees at that company. I'm sure they got workers who had no other options, but such an attitude isn't good for attracting and retaining employees. My conclusion on this is that the right answer is a tough one. Try to keep in the middle ground where employees feel safe coming to work, but common sense is still the rule of the day.

Why do I conclude that trust is a necessary ingredient? It's because you end up with better innovation at less cost. How can you argue with that? Employees who are not trusted will not do their best. Running a company out of fear will lead to much wasted time and low productivity. And costs in a fear-based organization are several times higher than in a trust-based organization. I value trust because I feel that it is critical to being successful.

5. Need a Vehicle

This is a principle that many businessmen today have forgotten about. It might be different in other industries, but the only one I'm familiar with is agriculture, and I know both older and younger innovators in this field. A lot of my opinions come from reflecting about our string of inventions and what factors were responsible for them.

In the older days (let's say the sixties or seventies) the large OEMs would actually pay you something for an invention. The inventor of one of our flagship products was actually the beneficiary of such an arrangement. I'm familiar with at least two of his inventions where he received a royalty for every one they produced. He would go to them with an idea and they would play fair, and he would receive a royalty that was fair. An inventor could actually be compensated for an idea without producing it in those days.

I had some personal experience with this same OEM some years later. Shortly before I hired on we evaluated an invention that a farmer had come up with. We were looking to license the invention from him if it worked. The OEM had also evaluated this invention. It turns out that the OEM filed their own patent application just days after they had evaluated the invention. I'm not saying that they had nothing additional to add to the patent, but it makes you wonder. Sure enough, the inventor didn't keep up on his maintenance fees, so in effect the OEM got the invention.

A few years later, we got a cease and desist letter from the same OEM saying that we had infringed on their issued patent. Luckily, we had filed our patent a couple weeks earlier than they had. We both had been issued patents due to a mistake on the part of the patent office. But we had the earlier filing date. One letter from our attorney and we never heard from them again on this issue. Sure, they had added some details to the invention that we weren't copying, so they had the right to a patent. But they shouldn't have been granted the claims they were. Why do I even mention these details? It's just that in the current business climate, you can't trust everyone. The chances of our being paid for our invention by someone licensing it are close to zero. We had to produce and sell a product in order to profit from our invention. It's difficult to make money any other way is this environment.

So what do I mean by a "vehicle"? A vehicle is something that you use to go somewhere. It's what you ride in from point A to point B. Point A is an idea. Point B is success in the marketplace. I was often the one who met with inventors to discuss their ideas and evaluate whether they had any value to Precision Planting. Most of these visits were a waste of time, but they were worthwhile in that we'd hate to miss the one person in a hundred who might have a good idea. And twice in our history our products have involved license payments to someone else for their patented idea. So the conclusion I've come away with is that in order to invent something of relevance, you need a vehicle to get it to production. Let's say you have a good idea and actually invent something, and let's say it's something that I'm going to put into production. I'll probably pay you 1-3% of the value as a royalty. You aren't going to make very much. And for that you need to spend a fair amount of money to get a patent issued and defend it. You might make some money in the end, but it's tough to retire rich.

There's just not a big enough market in agriculture for you to make millions.

But let me contrast this with the products we design, build, and sell. We mark them up so that typically they sell for around three times what it costs us to make them. But we have tooling to amortize, sales commissions to pay, and advertising to pay for. So it's not purely profit. At the end of the year we probably make a net 10-20% profit on these sorts of projects. The person who takes the risk makes ten times the earnings of the guy who has the great technical idea. Our vehicle is our products, brand, and dealer network. We have an established way of commercializing a new product idea.

But that's just the financial side of the equation. When I say you need a vehicle, what I mean is that you need an organization that is involved in the development and sales of a product to an end customer. The involvement with the customer has implications that aren't immediate. First, you understand if your current product is meeting the needs of the customer. Second, you understand what the marketplace needs for the future. Third, you're familiar with the tools of the industry, like stamping and molding processes, design and analysis tools, and so forth.

Let's elaborate on the first point. One of our products was called AirForce. The goal of this product was to get the correct force applied to the row unit so that it would plant at the proper depth. This was a product that our customers asked for. We were at our first sales conference trying to sell the ability we had just developed to measure the force on the gage wheels of the row unit. Every day, at least one customer would ask me when we were going to start controlling the force. Now that we could measure it, controlling it seemed like the next logical step to them. So that got me thinking that we ought to try selling a control system. By the next spring we were prototyping a control system, and it was a tad crude. But because we were in the market, we knew what the customer wanted and we were delivering it. The next spring we launched production in somewhat limited quantities. The quantity was limited but enough that we started to get real experience with it.

Over the next few seasons, I looked at a ton of data coming back from the field. I also walked a lot of our own fields and did scouting after we planted. From the data we had, I knew what the AirForce system was trying to do. On a few rows, I knew what we had actually achieved. I learned a bunch of things that would flavor my inspiration for our next product. I could see that not every row was the same, and we were going to need a product that could put an individualized amount of force on each row. I could also see that the ground hardness was changing faster than we could ever hope to control by using compressed air. I was seeing the weak points in our own design, through a combination of looking at the data and complaints we received from customers and walking our own fields. We had obviously made gains, and were better than the previous systems, but there was still room to improve.

So I started concept work on a system that would do what we truly needed for down-force. We started work on this two or three years before the market really started to scream for a better solution. In the same year that some of the competition started talking more about planter-wide hydraulic down-force, we announced row-by-row hydraulic down-force. We call this product DeltaForce. It is a custom cylinder on each row that has the control valve and plumbing integral to the cylinder. The market was starting to get more crowded in this area, but we were holding our own.

Now you could argue that I could have invented any of these products without being actively engaged in selling a product to a customer. But the chance of that is slim. Our AirForce product wasn't patented. It was just putting together a cost-effective system out of off-the-shelf components. It only had context for someone who was going to produce and sell the systems. There would be no way for some lone inventor to design the sheet metal, valves, and control systems for us to sell. It just doesn't work that way. That's why I say "You need a vehicle." We designed stuff that was only possible to do because we were active in the marketplace.

Regarding this last point, I recently had a conversation with one of our dealers about a product he'd envisioned. His idea would probably work, if a company could just figure out how to make it economically. He had a bunch of machined features that would be expensive and difficult. I had already done some brainstorming and was planning on molding these same features. Farmers are a cost-conscious bunch. It's not that they won't spend money when it's justified, but as an engineer you have to be judicious in how you design a product. Let's say for argument's sake that there are two design paths on a project. One might cost you $120 per row, the other $170 per row. I'm assuming the chance of success and robustness is the same with each design. The less expensive design can be sold for $350 per row. You'd have to sell the more expensive design for about $500 per row to make the same money. It's weird, but everything tends to scale with the cost: the commission to the dealer, the assembly, lots of things. And you'll sell a lot more at $350 than you will at $500. It's just a fact of life that if you're not practiced in the art of design, it's tough to be relevant to any manufacturer and design something they're going to want to build and sell.

I had the privilege of analyzing a startup company in a different industry. Their only business plan was to be acquired by someone big at a premium. They had no dealers. They had no sales. They had no revenue stream. Time has passed and I think they will be lucky enough to be acquired. But I have learned a lot by contrasting them with Precision. Because they have no revenue stream, they have been forced to give up a lot of equity and control. Because they have no product in the marketplace, their only hope is to be acquired. They are a hard company to value because there is nothing concrete to multiply.

If it were up to me, I'd start selling a product while looking for the suitor. I know it's two paths to focus on, but it provides a backup plan. It gives a vehicle if the other "ride" doesn't show up as hoped.

This subject ties into a later chapter as well about acting big. When you're engaged in production and have a vehicle of some size, it comes with the territory that you have larger production volumes. You can afford to design for processes that result in more professional-looking designs. And like it or not, most people are willing to buy that. They don't want to buy a part or system that looks like a prototype.

In conclusion, the people who are positioned to do the best job of innovating are those who are actively involved in selling a similar or the same product to the customer base. They have a "vehicle." They have a business, a brand, a sales force already in place. It's easy to work another product in. The danger of being in business is becoming complacent, and that's why innovation rarely comes from market leaders. But it rarely comes from total outsiders either.

6. Financing

This subject is related to the idea of a vehicle, but I made it its own chapter to draw attention to its importance. I know this runs contrary to the strategy that startups typically employ. Most startups have no products and no revenue stream. Precision, however, began with a product that provided seed money to start other ventures. My goal in writing this chapter is to get you thinking about your vision and how you want to spend your time and effort, before you get into one particular style too deeply.

There are two different ways to go about funding entrepreneurship. There is the classic way and then there's the home-grown way. Let me start with the classic approach to this topic.

An idea guy gets a brainstorm of a business plan. It will take a certain amount of funding to get it up and running. He has lots of friends, family, and business relationships. He spends most of his time calling on these people and convincing them that his ideas make sense and the idea will be profitable. They give him money to start putting these plans into motion. In exchange for funding, the idea guy gives up some control, in the form of shares of the company. Now the race is on. Spending the money (they call this the "burn rate") slowly enough to get the business running is always a challenge. Read any book by a serial entrepreneur and you'll find that they're always out of money or close to it. And they spend significant energy and effort either convincing others that they know what they're doing, or pleading for more money.

Once you've gotten some work done and spent the initial money you received from friends and family, you have to turn to venture capitalists—"vulture capitalists," as we call them affectionately in the business. I don't have experience with them, so I can't tell any good stories. But I know that control has to be given up to a great extent in order to take advantage of their capital. The idea is that they make lots of investments, knowing that many will go bust but that a few will hit it big.

Then there's the hope that a Prince Charming will come along and buy the business for big bucks so all the investors can be paid off. Many of these stories do not end so well. This is just a fact of life. The success rate for this model is not that high. And this is how the venture capital world plays out over and over again. Low probability of success (high risk) means that rewards for companies that actually make it might be high, but for each one that strikes it rich there are many that receive nothing or very little back on their investment.

Contrast this to a homegrown method of financing. Granted, this doesn't provide a super fast return. And it's not as fun to talk about owning a company for twenty years as it is to boast that you sold off your startup after three. But in the end, does it really matter? If what we're striving for is a successful business, then please consider the alternative.

I already mentioned that Precision was started in order to market a device called the Keeton Seed Firmer. This created a revenue stream that made the company solvent from the beginning. I wasn't involved in all the financial details, so I couldn't share them even if I wanted to. But I know a couple things. First, we had to borrow money from time to time. We weren't so rich that we could float everything ourselves. But these loans were ordinary business loans, not off-the-charts-risky loans from venture capitalists. The second thing I know is that the profits from the business were re-invested in the business. In my mind, this was crucial to much of the success we had.

Gregg knew that the ideas we had would keep bearing fruit. Each time we had a successful idea, those profits were used to fund the research into the next idea. This had to be done multiple times over. You can't stop after a single idea and start skimming the profits. This is as important, and as difficult, as a teenager learning to delay gratification. It's about work preceding reward. This isn't a natural impulse for most humans. We want instant reward. We want to enjoy the fruits of our labors right away.

I'm not a psychology expert, but I'm familiar with a few studies that show the truth of this principle. One famous one is the marshmallow study, conducted in the 1960s and 1970s by Walter Mischel at Stanford University. Mischel looked at young children and their ability to delay the gratification of eating a single marshmallow in exchange for two marshmallows a few minutes later. The ability to delay gratification carried through, as decades later these same people were still able to delay reward. Mischel didn't measure how many businesses they started, but rather characteristics that we all would agree make a person more likely to be successful. The point is obvious. You have to make a sacrifice in the short term in order to be successful in the long term. Once your business gets going, there will be plenty of time to enjoy the fruits of your success.

I think there are a couple reasons why this homegrown method of financing contributed to our success. First, I can say that the amount of time Gregg spent courting others for money was near zero. I remember one time we courted a large company to get money in order to fund a project. We spent a fair amount of time getting ready for the show and getting our act in line. Looking back, that might have been the right decision but it is hard to say for sure. We spent time that should have been spent on the commercial side of the equation. If we'd done that, we would have seen that the project was not as feasible as we thought. It was early on in our history and we weren't as good at considering all factors of a project early on. In the end, we were not successful at getting any money to fund the project. Fundamentally, we did learn a bit from this project that was useful in later projects. But we never commercialized the product as we were envisioning it. The ultimate reason was one technical flaw that we couldn't overcome. There were other projects like this that failed for technical reasons. But this was before we'd really honed our business analysis and learned to scrap projects early in the research phase if they didn't have good line-of-sight to being profitable. I'm not down on this project overall, since we learned things we could use later on, but it isn't the example I would use to illustrate how to do product development well. The point is that we wasted little time trying to obtain funding from others. In the big picture, it was fractions of a percent of the time we spent on product development as a whole.

The second advantage to growing a business in an organic mode is that of control. There was never a time where Gregg had to argue or convince anyone where the company was going. As long as the family was in agreement around the dinner table, things were settled. Funding comes with strings attached, generally in the form of stock. In exchange for money, you have to give up a degree of control. In our case, with a business that is also its own customer, staying control is an advantage. Maybe for some companies that aren't as connected to their customer base, it doesn't matter whether a single person can quickly and efficiently direct the organization. But if you're a company and a customer at the same time, you'll benefit greatly from having a leader who can make quick decisions without having to take the time to build a consensus.

7. Act Big

This is one principle that trips up many small businessmen. It might be risky to look at things this way. But it's also risky to look at things as many small companies do. To put it simply, you have to act like you're a bigger and more successful company than you really are. I'm not talking about the way you treat customers or suppliers. You always treat them with as much humility as you can. What I'm talking about is the way you advertise and the way you design your booth at a trade show.

I saw some of these companies peddling their wares at the national farm show. Ten years go by and they look the same. They still come across as a farmer making something out of his shop and selling it from the kitchen table. The brochure looks like it was designed in the 1970s and copied on the grade school mimeograph machine. You know that if you decide to do business with this company, you're going to have to put up with some level of—I don't know how else to put it—"hill-billy phone support." This company will always be what they are today. It's a self-fulfilling prophecy. They only attract a following that can identify with them. Everyone wants to dream that they're more sophisticated than they really are, so they'll always get a really small crowd of customers if they shoot at that level.

So how did Precision succeed? Even when it was a ten-foot booth, it was done with the highest degree of professionalism. Gregg got where he was through his ability to relate to farmers and talk one-on-one with them. But they never left the booth thinking, "Where is that guy going?" They knew the company was for real since Gregg had risked the money to buy a professional-looking stand. You might think this is risky, spending money before you've earned it to project an image you don't quite deserve yet. But there is also a risk that comes from being too cautious. You might lose half your potential customers if you have a dirty, dated display. I hold with the universally acknowledged truism about risk: Reward is in proportion to risk taken. Don't get me wrong, I'm not talking about taking reckless risks. But calculated, reasonable risks must be taken. Just sitting back and playing it safe isn't going to make your business succeed.

Over the eleven years I worked at Precision, I saw the company go from a small thirty-foot booth to multiple booths at the national show. One of the booths covered both sides of the aisle instead of just one. I might be biased, but I think our booth was one of the most crowded at the shows. We had farmers stop in the aisles and wait there to talk to one of us in the "white shirts." We fostered the impression that this was a company one ought to be associated with and learn from. We always focused on displays that would teach problems and solutions. We had excited employees. I could spend a whole chapter complaining about booths with employees absent or just sitting back, waiting for customers to engage them. But I think you get the point. Be professional, project the message that you're for real, and customers will come.

We launched a "mobile marketing" truck, a semi-trailer that opened up into a mobile classroom with many hands-on demonstrations. This truck and its support staff toured the country doing presentations in dealers' lots. You might say that this was too ambitious given our size, and you're probably right. But Gregg was always a visionary, and this strategy enabled us to grow to a size at which it was justified. As time went on, no one could argue with our using a truck in this way. Of course, we thought we were nuts early on, but pretty soon we saw the wisdom of this method.

So to conclude, have a little vision. Take a calculated risk. And don't short yourself when it comes to presenting the right image of where you're going in the marketplace. Today's customer is demanding, and eager to align with a perceived leader in the industry.

8. The Vanishing Organizational Chart

This may surprise you, but in all the history of Precision, we never once wrote down an organizational chart. Gregg's philosophy was that we did whatever needed to be done. He had a big fear of titles and organizational charts. This was something I never really understood till later in my career. There were two sides to this coin. It was tough sometimes to get as much done when you were working outside the company. Many people are used to looking at someone's title to ascertain their authority to make decisions. So I'll admit there were times when I wished we had some official titles. It would have made sense to have titles on our business cards that were wide-ranging in scope. That would have gotten other people's attention and helped us get things done when we needed to influence others. But I saw the advantage of this mindset when I had the opportunity to compare Precision to a large organization.

It seemed that many people in this organization were fixated on the org chart and how many people they had underneath them. And the amount of organizational energy that goes into shuffling the deck, so to speak, is amazing. It's a drag on efficiency and the organization as a whole. But I'm sure that there's a practical limit to the size of an organization that can function without some structure. There are advantages when it comes to keeping pay in sync across departments. There are advantages when an organization gets to larger sizes. But this is why smaller departments have the advantage when it comes to innovating. They're not shackled by any constraints on who does what or what responsibility a given person has.

Here's what you don't want: employees who are fixated on how to get ahead politically. You want to eliminate any focus on this. One example is pay. If you know what someone else is getting paid just from their position, you can start to feel jealous. There's the temptation to compare what you do, and how much value you create, to other people in the organization. You want it to be clear that pay is related to responsibility and value creation, and nothing else. This will incentivize correct behavior.

Large organizations do need org charts for certain purposes. Some tasks need to be divided up. Reviews need to be done from time to time. It doesn't work if a single person has hundreds of reviews to do. If you don't trust your employees, there will be expense reports and so on that need to be approved. There are legitimate reasons for organizational structure.

What you want is for the work and the decisions to be made at a low level. If every decision has to move up the org chart and back down, lots of time is wasted. You want a nimble organization. Let me describe how we did this at Precision as we were acquired and had to implement an organizational chart. We had a reporting structure. This structure was arranged in a functional way, not by project. For example, I had mechanical engineers reporting to me. But I wasn't involved in every detail of their projects. I knew generally what they were working on and might get involved in the details as the situation warranted. But they still made decisions in their project teams and moved quickly. Because they had similar backgrounds and were mechanical engineers, I could mentor them and give career advice. I had been through many of the same things. The most important principle in all of this is to keep the organizational chart from dragging down the speed at which you innovate and get projects done.

9. Engineers at the Helm

Who took the lead in product strategy and brainstormed future projects at Precision? To be fair, marketing sometimes put in requests for products. But these were more along the lines of categories than specific requests. For example, marketing might say to us, "We need something to sell to John Deere vacuum planter owners," because it was a market we had neglected in the past. Eventually we served that market well, but not because we forced a product upon it. It was because we came to appreciate the market's existing weaknesses and relieved the customers' pain. All of our product ideas came from a true understanding of how planters actually worked, and by attacking problems and coming up with great solutions. As a result, the ideas came from engineering and were driven at that level, instead of having marketers and bureaucrats lay out the product roadmap.

Once we were fishing for a new product, and the starting point was data we gathered in the tractor cab in order to really understand how planters worked. We had a prototype on a laptop that was reporting the meter performance and spacing on every row. When Gregg saw how we could monitor the planter in real time, he realized that every farmer would want this. They currently had lights that told them whether they were planting or not, but little else. In this way an idea was born. The product was a planter monitor, and it came from measuring the performance of the planter in order to invent a product. It was funny how that worked. In the process of gathering data in order to understand the weaknesses in the existing technology, we came up with a product idea, which became a significant product and even a family of products for Precision. We spent many years working on this product and on extensions of it.

Many product ideas came as a result of measuring accuracy. I'm convinced that improved data measurement and acquisition goes hand in hand with the invention of better mechanical devices. CleanSweep was a product born from our experience being the customer. 20/20, a planting monitor that gives farmers real-time planter performance information, was conceived as a result of engineering having a prototype measurement system in the cab. AirForce was a product that our customers asked for. DeltaForce came from working with a previous product in the field. We didn't need a bunch of marketing guys to manage a list of features and compare us with the competition. We weren't competing by doing things a little bit better. We were making new categories of products. We were leading the market. We had nothing against our marketing guys. It's just that they weren't in the position to connect the dots and come up with product ideas the way our engineers were. Keep in mind that this doesn't work unless your engineers are also customers. Take traditional engineers, isolate them from the customers, and this strategy will fail miserably. We made it work because we engineers farmed, spent a lot of time talking directly to farmers, or spent lots of time in the cab of a tractor dreaming up ideas with farmers.

And then there's the reality of the day-to-day decisions that engineers make. If they're customers as well, they have the information they need to make the right decisions. If they're just engineers, they have to ask someone questions about every decision. This became very apparent to us when we were working with a large OEM on a project. We had a few questions about product usage, and we knew that by going to a couple of our regional managers we would get an immediate answer. Our regional managers knew what the customer needed and immediately they both gave us the same answer. By contrast, at the OEM, the engineers had to "talk with the commercial team." After a week they came back with an answer different from the one we figured out, one that made no sense. They were too disconnected from the customer to even arrive at the correct specification for how the product would perform. It's no wonder that their products were not performing at industry-leading levels. If you don't understand the problem correctly, how can you fix it?

It goes without saying that you don't have to micromanage these sorts of engineers. There's a certain freedom that engineers feel when they can do their own work without having every detail spelled out for them. You save quite a bit of management time in planning projects. The engineers feel like they have some say or control on their own projects. This is probably a bigger deal to most engineers than we tend to realize.

So this is the attitude that prevails at all levels at Precision. There are a few engineers who are not farmers, but most have some connection to farming, either through Gregg's farm or their own family farm. Our engineers didn't have to waste time looking for someone who understood the customer. They were usually the customer themselves as well. And this resulted in two things: products that got the little details right, and products that in the big picture were what the customer needed.

One thing that you wouldn't find at Precision was people who didn't understand our customer but got their position through seniority. This was partially a function of being a young company. I'm convinced, though, that this principle would never have taken hold no matter how old Precision got. As I've said before, you want as many decisions as possible made at a low level. We pushed most responsibility for making decisions as low as possible. It's about engaging people. There's nothing as demotivating as wasting a bunch of time while decisions are routed up the food chain to people who don't know enough to make a good decision. Of course, there are some decisions that need to be made at a high level. But these should only be strategic decisions. And these kinds of strategic decisions should be made by senior people. Of course, when decisions like these are made, it's good for there to be agreement at all levels throughout the organization. There will be less in-fighting if these sorts of decisions are agreed upon in the early phase of a project. Everyone will be in alignment, working towards the same goals.

Part II

Technical Acumen

10. Cut It Open

This is one principle that you might get a chuckle out of. And it's one of the most important from a technical standpoint.

When grappling with a problem, you need to be able to get quickly to the root cause. I've seen engineers run test after test and then try to describe how the system works using the test results. But if you can't explain the physical phenomenon at the root of the test results, you'll rarely get to the right answer, and if you do it will take longer.

My first story comes from working night shift at Caterpillar. We were building some off-highway trucks that we called pilots, and they were intended to be hydraulically different. The engines and transmissions were supposed to be the same. They called me to do a pressure check because the brake cooling pressures were not measuring correctly. I put pressure taps in everywhere I could, and finally traced the problem to something inside a brake cooler. I told the mechanics to pull the cooler off the engine. There was nothing to ID the part on it anywhere that I could find. So finally I decided that we were going to cut this thing in half and see what was wrong on the inside. I threw the cooler on my bike and rode over to the prove design shop. I found a guy running a bandsaw and told him to split it down the middle. I think he thought I was nuts. But once he cut it open, I immediately saw the problem. They had installed a 9 baffle instead of a 5 baffle oil cooler. They had both on the line at the engine plant, and for some reason they'd grabbed the wrong one. They were the same size in every other respect, so nothing gave it away. By that point I could tell the engine plant what they were doing wrong, and it was easy to fix. You might think this was weird, but just think of how many hours we'd have spent trying to figure out the problem normally. I'd call a meeting, we'd discuss options. An engineer at the engine plant might discover the error, but they only built a few such brake coolers, so the likelihood of the mistake being noticed was slim. Then we'd meet again to decide if we'd found the problem or not. All this versus the expense of one oil cooler down the drain. Quick answers and the correct ones are what pay off.

Recently a similar story happened at Precision, when one of our engineers was testing out some prototype valve/hydraulic cylinder combos. Nearly all of them had blown a seal down where the valve mated into its cavity. He just put one on the bandsaw and sawed it open. Immediately he could measure the cavity and figure out that it was not machined correctly. I just had to smile. This was the same "get to the root cause" attitude that I've always believed in. It results in quick, correct answers. I wish everything could be cut open and measured, it would save a lot of time. It's fine to hypothesize and come up with ways to test the hypothesis, but I've seen these sorts of problems often turn into weeks or months of experimentation.

Let me illustrate the more common but less obvious scenario where this presents itself. A little instruction in meter performance is required. We do a lot of work trying to optimize "singulation" of a meter. There are two things that converge in the definition of singulation: skips and doubles. A skip is the lack of a seed on a hole of the disk. A double is where there are two seeds stuck where there should only be one. It's very possible when running a test to conclude that singulation is about the same regardless of speed. Or you might change the vacuum between two tests and conclude that singulation is the same. But if you look closer at the data, you see that doubles are causing the problem one time and skips are causing the problem another time. Now, if it's the same dimension causing the problem in both cases, it may be tough to solve. But if the doubles are coming because of one feature, and the skips are coming because of another, then two changes may solve both problems. That's why I get kind of worked up when I'm given data about something but no theory about the cause or explanation of the physics that makes sense. I've become convinced that if you don't push for the root cause, you're just guessing at the solution regardless of how much data you have.

I have to wonder how many problems have gone unsolved because the root cause wasn't properly identified. Some test was run, a conclusion was drawn, but the problem wasn't fully understood. Getting a good view of the problem with the high-speed camera turned out to be a really valuable exercise. Many, many times we were unsure of what was going on. One of the first engineering tools we invested in was a high-speed camera. At the time, a used demo model cost $15,000. It only worked in black and white, but it was amazing what we did with that. We agonized over that decision. We had our best negotiator work with the guy after I said it was what I wanted. But when I looked back on that decision a few years later, I saw it was one of the best ones we made. We got to where we could actually see what was going on, and learned so much. We got really good at cutting something apart, putting Plexiglas windows in place, and taking video of the parts in motion. It became a real challenge on some designs, but we knew that if we could accomplish it, we'd get to an answer.

I remember one recent example. We had a product that we couldn't get a good view into. I'd been out of the design details for some time, so this was a little bit of a stretch. But I took a few days and made some design changes so that we could have parts built and see into the design. The end result was that we could see the wheels that were actually grabbing the seed. The alternative was just to see the downstream measurement by the sensor. This was a case where the investment up front was larger than some. But the result was that you could directly see what effect the design changes were having. This kind of action both helps the engineer reach a solution more easily, and lets him communicate its effectiveness much easier to those in management.

I can't overemphasize the importance of focusing on the root cause. I have to remind myself again and again that it's always worth the effort. It's tempting just to take a simple test result and infer success, but if we can really see what's going on, it helps so much. Using the camera and cutting a design open have been crucial in this respect.

Marketing even used the videos from the high-speed camera to sell our products. And we took a gutsy approach in that we did many presentations live onstage. I remember working with Gregg, trying to get a mistake to happen in front of hundreds of customers. Then I'd play the video in slow motion to show what problem had just occurred. It was easy to show that our solution was the fix. Nobody can argue with actually seeing a problem and its solution in action.

11. Vertical Integration

I'm sure that many people will object to the idea I'm about to put forth. It runs counter to what you've been taught in class. And some of it comes from economics theory. Though this principle can be taken too far, I believe that in general everyone should do what they're best at. Let me illustrate this with a hypothetical project in a large organization. You have the design engineer, and all he does is orchestrate, schedule meetings, and make sure everyone is on the same page. Then you have someone who does the design work in some solid modeling package, such as pro/ENGINEER or SOLIDWORKS. You have a detailer who mocks up all the drawings. You have a manufacturing representative who is supposed to bring manufacturing issues to meetings and evaluate how difficult it is to assemble or repair the design. Then you have someone who builds the prototypes and someone who tests them. Never mind the representative from the molder or machine shop who is going to actually make the parts. It's easy to get eight or more different functions involved on even a small project. There are so many opportunities for mistakes when using this model. Every hand-off is an opportunity to forget to mention some "little" detail. One of the keys to successful products is in the little details. You've got to get them right if you want to have success early on. The market might excuse mistakes once you're the leader, but in order to truly innovate, you have to be right.

And then there's the whole subject of detailing. When I was at CAT in the early days, we had a group that did detailing. The idea was that we engineers were supposed to do the design work, then we'd throw the designs over the wall to a detailer. It wasn't uncommon for detailing to assign a hundred hours or more to lines group. I was the engineer on hydraulics, and there might be fifteen hoses plus clips and all the fittings and seals and hardware in a lines group. And it would take me ten or twelve hours of checking and putting red marks on these drawings to get them done. Or I could do the detailing myself in eight hours. So it was an obvious choice. I just did the work myself. But it got better than that. When we were making some changes in personnel, I got one of the better detailers and told him he was doing design under my direction. It took me a little work to teach him, but he learned to do the line routing in pro/ENGINEER. Then, when it came time to do the detailing, he could do it quickly, as he didn't have to learn what he was working with. So we got a lot more work done with a lot fewer hours billed to our project. I was working on a few groups doing design and detailing, and he had a couple other groups and did design and detailing. And we did it by throwing conventional wisdom on its head. Now you've got to keep your mind about you. You can spend too much time working in the shop, doing some job that it doesn't really pay to have the engineer doing. But most of the time it pays to have as few people working on the job as possible and each person understanding as much as possible about how the whole story fits together.

Now let's picture another alternative to the conventional way of working. An engineer understands the various manufacturing processes at play in his design. He quickly designs the parts himself in a solid modeling program. Then he makes some of them himself, or has them outsourced, depending upon complexity and in-house capability. For example, it's not worth outsourcing if it will take two hours to make phone calls, email prints around in order to decide on who gets the job, and write a PO, when he can just make the parts he needs in an hour himself. So maybe he isn't the best machinist and someone else could do the job in half an hour. But that's irrelevant to his decision and only comes into play when the team as a whole is doing so much machining that a machinist is justified. Then the engineer puts the parts together himself, or maybe with a little shop help. He experiences the problems with assembly himself. This is opposed to the alternative: Someone else forgets to tell him that there was a certain problem putting the design together. And then this engineer knows what works and what doesn't after he has built the first version of his design.

The benefits don't stop in the design cycle alone. Think about field testing and production startup. Early experiences with the field are hard to beat. They teach your product designers so much. Yes, there is a place for the product support team in this process. But there is no substitute for the engineer taking a phone call from the customer. The goal is not just this product, but the long term. You can't hope to educate and form good habits in your engineers from second- or third-hand experiences.

Early on we had to bet the farm. We released products whose readiness for commercial production was debatable. We were able to get through it by taking care of customers and replacing products. But when we talked to customers and felt the pain they were feeling, it influenced our future decisions. Want to take a risk with something that affects reliability? Remember the time you tried to explain to the customer why he had to stop every round to clean out his meter disk? These are priceless learning opportunities. As a practical matter, we would put the design engineer right in the middle of the phone team. He would have a good pulse on what types of calls we were receiving. He would teach the other members how to deal with the simple problems, and focus on the tougher problems himself. Together we'd hold things together and get to the bottom of the technical issues. Remember, it's not just about being "efficient" with every moment of an engineer's time. It's about getting the project done well and in minimal calendar time. It's easy to forget this the more you analyze and track people's time.

Another reason this is beneficial is the camaraderie of the whole organization. I wish it weren't this way, but there's a tendency among departments to play the blame game. This doesn't happen in small organizations, but as the company grows, it takes more effort to overcome. When the chips are down, no one likes to be abandoned. Picture a few guys in product support taking phone calls with no engineering support. They can get discouraged pretty quickly. Now imagine that a couple engineers have moved in with them temporarily and are helping diagnose problems. Their attitude will be much better. Both can feed off of each other and help each other in making the project successful. In the end there's a feeling of trust and respect for each other that will help on future projects as well.

One example of this is our RowFlow product introduction. RowFlow is a seeding control system that controls hydraulic motors for variable rate planting and also controls row clutches for row shutoffs. We had many problems with wiring harness construction and quality. Our product team and sales were floundering, feeling like we in engineering didn't care. A couple of engineers moved in and sat with our phone team for a month. They helped in diagnosing the problems and talking on the phone to customers. This changed the attitude quickly. They felt like we were working together to solve the problems and make things better.

What I've talked about till this point deals mostly with the direct hours of the project and the costs involved. But there's another intangible part of this story. And that's the communication involved. The fewer people involved in a project, the smaller the chance that someone forgets to communicate something important. For example, someone is testing a meter. If he's the same one who's doing the design, chances are he won't forget what he saw while testing when he goes back to work on the design. Now it makes sense to use some help getting the test set up and doing some of the work. But you, the engineer, should participate in the testing to the point that you learn and see the key findings. If you're an engineer who's stuck to his desk because you're hung up on yourself and your degree, good luck getting any good designs off that desk. It's just one of those facts you can't get around: The more people involved in something, the more chances of miscommunication.

Let's recap the theme of this chapter: You want people on your teams who have the widest variety of skills possible. For smaller projects, if a single person can do it, then the outcome will be better. Of course, this assumes you have good people. And I don't take anything away from brainstorming and log-jam breaking by others. There are times when even the best engineer is stuck and just needs to run things by someone else. But the value of that collaboration is high and doesn't involve the drag of having lots of people working on the project. One-off advice doesn't have the negative impact that comes with multiple people trying to work together over the long term. Keep your head about you, and do every task with as few people as possible. You'll have the best outcomes. That's what managing for innovation is about.

One of the principal reasons for having good employees is the reduced need for communication. The number of communication channels on a particular project is expressed by this formula:

$C = N*(N-1)$

What we see here is that the number of communication channels grows exponentially as the number of people on a project grows. What we mean by a communication channel is a path of communication between two people. It means, for example, the hardware engineer talking to the software engineer about the specification for a chip. It means the packaging engineer talking with the software engineer about the style of connector he wants to use. As more and more people are added to the project, the amount of time spent communicating with one another starts to become overwhelming. This is one reason why good people and as few of them as possible are the ideal solution for getting a project done.

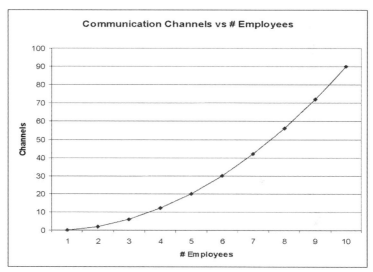

Simple chart to illustrate communication channels and the need to keep teams small.

In conclusion, you want teams of highly skilled engineers who are capable of filling as many roles as possible. This results in fewer hand-offs that present opportunities for fumbles. This ensures that communication needs are minimized and important details aren't forgotten. It isn't conventional, but vertical integration is a concept that can really pay dividends.

12. He Who Tries the Most Things Wins

This chapter might seem obvious to many of you. But I've found it's not obvious to most engineers. I'm talking about times when you're stumped, when you're unable to solve a problem. I'm not talking about the times when you need to shoot the engineer and go to production.

Much of our work over the years focused on raw invention and problem solving. There were times when we were really stumped. The problems we were working on were new to us. So we hadn't yet developed that gut instinct that told us what would work and what wouldn't work. There are a couple choices in this situation. You can become paralyzed and not do anything. Or you can start trying things. Test something. Build something. You'll probably learn something. It might not be the end solution you uncover. But in order to get to a solution, you have to understand how things work. And oftentimes this picture is built by putting lots of little pieces together. You can't figure out the little pieces if you're afraid of making a mistake.

Probably the defining moment in my understanding of this was on a project we called PopMax. PopMax is a replacement part for a type of meter—it's a special backing plate that improves performance. It was a high-wear item that was previously made by stamping, heat-treating, and then chrome-plating steel. Even so, this part would only last a few years, depending upon the severity of the environmental conditions. The funniest part of this was during the first attempt at re-engineering this part.

Our molder told us our biggest problem would be that we would never sell another part again once we sold a customer the first one. It would last so long out of nylon, and we'd never need to replace it. Turns out this is a case where one experiment is worth thousands of opinions. We tested it, and it did fine. We sold a bunch of them to customers. In some cases, they wore out in a day or two. We found that in real life there's abrasive dust that we never used in our testing. You just can't substitute lab conditions for real field conditions. Once you've run a part in real field conditions, you can sort of calibrate your test stand conditions. Without that, you're totally guessing at how aggressive to be with your testing.

So we started looking for alternatives from a design standpoint. For every option we tried, someone was sure that it would totally fix the problem. For every option, someone else would have told us a reason it wouldn't work. In a few days, I could tell whether some solution had any hope of working. I did this by testing on our endurance test stand. Many of these "solutions" failed in a single night. It was just easier to run the test and have an answer than argue. Many engineers would like to have numerous meetings to discuss and debate what was going to be the best solution. But I found it was best to just simply try. And you know what? We learned about every treatment, coating, and hardening method out there. An hour on the phone, a couple weeks waiting for samples, and we knew the strengths and weaknesses of each process. Some of this was "wasted" time for this project, but much of it we used over the years on other projects. We learned a lot about wear and materials from this testing.

So that's why I don't discourage testing and experimentation. At this point I have enough of a gut feeling that we don't need to do quite as exhaustive a search when working on some new application. But I'm slow to tell the guys to cut the engineering short. I've just found that time spent trying things in the lab is how you learn, and you rarely learn anything by arguing at a whiteboard.

To illustrate this point, here's a project I was involved in over the last few weeks. One engineer had a theory of what was causing a particular problem and how to solve it. I wasn't following him and thought his understanding didn't make sense. Now this was an easy idea to test. A few hours in the test stand would prove whether this idea was correct or not. So it was an easy choice to make. We could either spend a few hours in the conference room arguing about theory and physics, or we could just test the idea in a few hours in the lab and know for sure. In the end, we just tried it out and proved it wouldn't work. This is one reason I'm quick to try stuff, especially if it's easy and the results aren't known from past experience.

Lest you get the wrong idea, I certainly realize there's a time to "shoot the engineer" on most projects. This probably deserves a chapter or book of its own, in reality. I'll try to cover the basics in just a few paragraphs.

Rarely has the most successful product in the marketplace been the perfect product from a technical standpoint. Continuing to keep a project in the engineering stages can be the death of a company. Products succeed not because they're theoretically perfect, but rather because they fill a blend of needs. You can get overly focused on any one aspect and miss the others. You need to have a certain mixture of a few basic things.

First, there must be a financial impact that's positive for the customer. We tried to develop products that paid for themselves in a fraction of one planting season. Very few people could argue with the money side of our products. And this wasn't as much actual field testing with documented results as it was a plausible explanation. Maybe it's a product to improve meter performance. Let's say you get a 1% improvement. That would come out to two bushels per acre, which is $10 roughly (at $5/corn). Each row plants about 100 acres of corn, so it's worth potentially $1000 per row. If the product only costs $100 per row, your financial analysis is good enough. You don't have to worry about the decimal points and argue with the customer. It's hard for him to knock down the value enough in his mind to reach the point when it won't pay off. So what if he only gets one quarter the return he expected? It's still paying for itself in the first year.

And then it has to solve a problem that's easy to understand. Some of our early products were simple mechanical things. One was a seed belt that centered the seed. When a farmer saw that one part, he could easily grasp that it was different and had to be better. And it cost him about $10. It was easy to sell products like this. And it exactly replaced a part he was replacing every few years anyway. It's hard to keep a customer's attention when the marketing story is long and difficult. You want it easy to understand and simple for him to get.

The final part is making the customer's life easier. I often say that "farmer" is spelled L-A-Z-Y, but in reality I think we're all that way. Who wants a product that is confusing to use and results in you, the customer, being unsure if you're using it correctly? There needs to be a feature in your product that hits the personal side of things. It just needs to be Brain Dead Simple. If not, you'll struggle to ever move beyond the early adopters who are willing to put up with lots of nonsense in order to have a better system.

If you hit those three areas, you have a winner. Stand back and watch the orders pour in.

So what's the conclusion? If you have a project that's offering improvement in a few areas and it's successful in terms of life expectancy, then get the engineers out of the way and go to production. If you're stuck with a serious problem and can't find solutions, don't be afraid to try things. And try as many different solutions as possible.

13. Picket Fence Intellectual Property

This one's easy to write about. I think our approach to intellectual property was unique at Precision, because we were a small company. Intellectual property rights pertain to a few different areas. The first is getting clearance to produce a design without infringing on others' rights. This involves understanding the landscape and who has what ideas patented. The second is protection to make your own design. The third is stopping others from copying your products. We had a unique way of doing this well. I learned everything I could about patents. We had a good attorney who advised us, filed everything, and oversaw all the work. He was a good teacher, and he taught me how to read a patent, how to analyze the claims, and even how to write them. We figured out it was fastest if I wrote the first-pass provisional patent, then he cleaned things up for the final filing. I would even do the claims structure in layman's terms, and he would double-check my strategy and put things in legal language. It was a good combination. Eventually we got large enough that I fell behind in getting enough applications filed. So we hired our own patent attorney and started catching up as quickly as we could.

When we were bought out, part of the analysis that was done was of our patents. And I heard anecdotally that we had one of the best IP platforms they had ever analyzed. I don't take credit for this myself. It was the combination of an excellent attorney who taught me, as well as putting the strategy in the hands of someone who understood the industry. This was another area where Gregg wasn't afraid to spend serious money for good counsel. I'm sure we could have gotten cheaper advice per hour, but we wouldn't have learned as much, and the end result wouldn't have been the same.

Let me describe what I've seen done by companies that are smaller in size, or even by lone inventors. What typically happens is that after an invention is complete, a prototype is given to a small-town attorney. He has probably filed a few patents in his spare time between domestic court cases. He covers the invention as he sees it in his claims. The client reviews the work and, because he is unfamiliar with legal writing, fixes a couple technical details but is lost as to the whole point of the claims. These patents are easily identifiable. They have poorly written claims that are easy to get around. We ran into more than a few of this type of patent over the years.

Contrast this with our winning strategy for IP. You start by scoping out the industry. Ideally, your design engineer or project lead does this. You figure out up front if there are any areas you need to avoid. Redesigning a product at the end is expensive and wastes a lot of time. You might not get a formal clearance opinion, but at least you learn what's been published. Then you can go to work designing your product. This might take you some time, or it might be easy. It all depends on the product. Once you've gotten to the proof-of-concept stage, it's time to do a little review. You make sure that you aren't infringing on anyone's patents, now that you know what your product looks like. And you can make an outline of what IP you hope to get at this point. This is where your way of thinking becomes important. You have to think like a competitor, someone who's trying to get around your patent. You understand the product well, and what features are most critical to its success. And you build your claims and strategy accordingly. You want to make sure to block off every angle from which someone might try to copy your design.

You won't always be lucky enough to do this. I'm talking here about patents we're hoping to get issued. The whole package is still working its way through the patent office, and then we'll have to defend these patents as well, which will be just the beginning of the money we have to spend.

We worked hard to try to keep others from infringing on our intellectual property and we always tried to get several broad areas of protection. The first would be on the design of any mechanical components. There are easy ways around this type of patent. It really only keeps someone from making a dead copy. That's where a lot of people would stop, though, and it's worth something because it keeps other people from preventing us from building our own design.

So let's say someone gets around our mechanical design, which is easy to do. We patented that basically so that people would have to work to copy us. It takes real engineers to come up with an original design. It's easy to copy someone else's. You actually don't need much in the way of engineers. You can just take a part to many contract suppliers, and they can build you a copy just by looking at a design. That's why you want to get a patent on the mechanical details.

Many of our products are more than mechanical parts. So, if possible, we would also file claims in a separate patent on how we analyzed or used data gathered in the product. This would require a copycat to not only use a different mechanical design, but also analyze data separately at the end of the day. Depending on the complexity involved, it might work or it might not. There are sometimes multiple ways to solve a problem, but sometimes a certain way is the best. If marketing is good, they can come up with reasons why your way is best that resonate with the customer, and this becomes a real advantage, regardless of what the whole truth is.

Finally, if the product contained a user interface that presented information to the farmer, we would typically file another patent covering how the information was presented. This would put up another roadblock that would make it difficult for other companies to copy our product. Combined, it's what we mean by "picket fence" IP—it's a tough fence to get through. The pickets are close together. It's not one set of claims. It's multiple ones aimed at slightly different ways of getting the same result, which makes it really hard for a competitor to get through.

So, you can spend a lot of money to get these patents issued, and all they really give us is the right to spend more money to sue an infringer. But regardless of whether we end up having to do that or not, there's a very good reason to file applications on your designs. A few years back, we announced a product at a summer sales conference. The night before, we'd filed the patent describing our invention. Then, a year or two later, we got a cease and desist letter from another company. Right after they saw our announcement, they'd applied for a patent for basically the same design, with a few details added. Fortunately for us we had the first filing date. But if we hadn't filed a patent application in a timely fashion, we'd have ended up having to go to court to prove who'd invented it first, and that would have cost us in two areas. First, it would surely have been expensive. Second, there would have been an opportunity cost: we would have lost engineering time. The conclusion we came to was that it pays to have filed before announcing a new product. This was a lesson we heeded religiously on all future product rollouts.

14. In-source

This term means a couple things at Precision. We happened to have a supplier by that name. And this was one case, perhaps the only one, where giving engineering responsibility to someone outside of our organization actually worked. What I'm referring to here is having the in-house capability to do most things. But let me digress for a moment, and explain why in some cases we found partnering to be advantageous.

In the case of In-Source Technologies, I think we were successful because of the quality of the engineers at that company. Their lead engineer was one of the sharpest guys I've worked with. He contributed real solutions to the problems we were working on. It wasn't like many relationships. We didn't have to give guidance on every step. He'd actually come up with solutions himself—in that way, he functioned like an integral part of the team. Sure, we were always batting ideas back and forth, and we set the overall priority, but we didn't have to take ownership of each and every detail. Contrast that with a couple projects they did for us that didn't go as well. The engineers involved weren't as experienced, so we had to micromanage them more. That is when the working relationship isn't going to be as smooth. Situations like those are best avoided if you want to innovate and do it quickly.

In general, I feel that you do the best job, and the quickest job, when your people understand what's going on. The time it takes to get a new person up to speed on a project is just too great. So let's spend a few minutes discussing contract employers and what they can bring to the table. It's just a fact that contract agencies generally have average or sub-par employees, and oftentimes it just doesn't work. We were usually short-handed on projects. I think we tried every contract agency in our area at one time or another. We always had high hopes, but it rarely worked out. The engineers would have some skills, I won't deny that. But their skill set was relatively narrow. We were just used to engineers who could do practically anything. We got caught in this trap so often. You couldn't afford to keep working with someone because they were taking too much time, but you couldn't afford to switch because the person you were using already knew too much. It was a catch-22. We just wished we'd listened to our better instincts and not gotten into that position in the first place. As far as dollars and cents go, it's certainly not efficient. You might get more done than you would without them, but for the money spent, the value received is poor. If you're cashed-strapped, this is surely not the way to get ahead.

Maybe this is just another way of saying you want the A-team. I think it's ultimately the same thing. With the company that we had great results with, we had the best of their minds on our projects. Some projects didn't go so well with them, but it came down to the particular people on the project. And when you go with contract companies, you don't typically get the best employees. The best people, the A players, are already employed and are rarely looking for work. Very few good engineers want to work in the contract agency environment. So it's just a reality that you'll rarely get good people by hiring contract workers.

Let me tell you about one project where we tried to use contract engineers. We were reverse-engineering a design and had a few design changes we wanted to make. So I sat down with the lead engineer and explained what we wanted to do. When I got the prototype and production parts, I had numerous mistakes to deal with. The impeller didn't fit on the shaft because the taper had been guessed, not measured and designed appropriately. Bolts didn't fit, and I never figured out why. Details were messed up in one of the complicated parts, requiring new tooling the following year. The way they did this design was that the lead engineer was onsite, and he took back much of the detailed work to the office to be done by a junior engineer. This was a recipe for disaster. Sure, I should've caught these mistakes, but I trusted them to simply copy a design. Turns out they couldn't even do that without mistakes. That's just one example of why I'm hesitant to use contract engineering firms. The buck always stopped with us, and I don't think they fixed any of these mistakes on their dime. If you don't have the time and resources to do it right the first time, I would suggest not attempting shortcuts.

It's not that we never used contract engineers. There were times when we had a job that was narrow in scope and whose duration was relatively short. And those were times where we might have used outside engineering. But I can say that if the role was at all strategic or long-term in nature, we were better off hiring a full-time person who met all our other requirements.

15. Effective Meetings

Our meetings weren't the typical meeting you picture at a large company. As we were smaller, we might have one structured meeting a week. I remember my wife being frustrated when we were first married, because most of the meetings at Precision weren't scheduled. The concept of a calendar was rather foreign to us. We just met when we needed to. Gregg would show up and we'd have a meeting. It wasn't conventional or by the book, but it worked, and that's how a small company functions.

As we got larger, it seemed like those of us who had leadership roles were in meetings most of the time. But the average design engineer attended one or two meetings a week to discuss the status of their project. To them, it was as if meetings had been eliminated. They came from a large company and were used to multiple meetings each day. On the largest project we had going, I did a whole team meeting every couple weeks or so. I had one meeting with each engineer once per week to discuss any important questions and review the status of his area. These were to-the-point, and everyone appreciated the conciseness of meetings like this.

So were the few meetings we had always productive? At times we weren't a model for effective meetings, but in recent years we honed this skill. We'd discuss items and make decisions. An hour or two of meeting time was all it took. We'd never heard of a multiple-day meeting. Then we were bought out and things changed. I'm not talking about internal R&D meetings, but rather meetings between the two entities. Luckily I wasn't there, but my brother tells me about multiple meetings where the introductions and non-meeting stuff would last a couple hours or more. And then there's the subject of the two-day meeting. It's hard to imagine what you can actually keep talking about for two days straight. Thankfully, we weren't wasting time, but we heard of meetings where the only conclusion reached was to meet again in a couple months. Granted, there are times where you stall someone and want to take months accomplishing little. But we just didn't have the time to waste in fruitless meetings. Our time was spent accomplishing things. Sharing data and making decisions. Moving the ball forward is the goal.

Right now, I'm involved in a meeting string on a new project with the larger organization that acquired Precision. Every couple months we have a meeting. In the first meeting, I said what we were planning to do and gave the timeline as it affected others. When this month's meeting came around, I contacted the organizer and said nothing had changed from our end, I was free but wouldn't take the few hours to call in unless needed. He said I wasn't needed and could skip. After the call, I got an email that said they wanted a different solution for the equipment. I gave a few suggestions but said we didn't have the resources to put much work into it right now. I heard nothing. Now I get an invitation to another meeting a few months from now. Nothing has happened on the equipment side that I'm aware of. I can't say how this will go. I predict that we'll have another meeting to hear that nothing has transpired. This is how large corporations operate. The attitude in a startup is different. It's focused on getting things done, on putting plans in place and executing them.

You can take whatever lessons from this that you want. The bottom line is, analyze how your people are spending their time and be sure they're not just sitting in meetings. Make sure they're spending most of their time doing real work and making real innovation happen. I came up with a saying that I now hear repeated quite often: Ivory-tower discussions aren't what get things done. We can have many debates in front of a whiteboard about what will be the winning design or the right answer. But no number of discussions or meetings will actually give us the answer. It takes an experiment or test in the lab or the field to answer many of these questions. That's why I'm all in favor of asking questions in a meeting and trying to frame the experiment, but at the same time I'm anxious to quit talking about it and start doing the experiment to get the answer. The proof is in the pudding, so to speak.

16. Electrons Too

All the anecdotes in this book so far have been from the mechanical side of things, where my experience lies. On the software side, we were innovative as well, but I was involved with software only a little at the strategic level, and none at the nuts and bolts level. My brother managed this side of Precision's R&D and was instrumental in guiding its development. We found that many of the principles in this area were the same as with mechanical products, but there are some differences. Understanding the customer is necessary for both. Timelines and the ability to change rapidly are different, though.

Let me start with our thinking about software and some of our successes. This effort really ramped up with our development of FieldView and FieldView Plus. FieldView is an iPad application that provides high definition planting and harvest maps and reports that farmers use for improved decision making. The only difference between the two products is the price and number of features. An annual subscription is charged for the premium features.

One way of developing a software product is to spend a couple months trying to detail everything out on a whiteboard. Then large teams of coders break down the work into chunks they will do. The testing is very involved, as it starts only after large chunks of work have been completed. By the time much of that work begins, either details have been forgotten or things have changed along the way. This could be due to marketing changes or things learned in early coding and development. Back to the whiteboard we go to discuss and rehash the project and how we should implement the code to accomplish our goals.

Contrast this with the agile way that we handled software development at Precision. We had a small team. People can't believe that the basic code was developed by just five people. And our program received recognition from Apple as one of their top apps for use on the iPad. There are a few more engineers than that now, but it's still a very small group. Of course, the vision of the project was a little more determined up front. But as far as details go, we would only discuss them maybe a couple weeks ahead of time. This kept time in meetings to a minimum. It meant that testing was broken into smaller chunks and could start sooner. It meant little time repeating things that had changed. If we got customer feedback the first year, we could roll that into future years more easily than if we had waited a few years, built every feature we could imagine, and then released it to the public.

I'm sure this isn't new to anyone in the software industry. There are numerous theories about agile development and how to develop rapidly. But when we hear stories from acquaintances about thousands of developers and years spent on a project, it makes us scratch our heads. Granted, we're starting with much smaller applications, but this mindset ought to be used for larger ones too.

Part III

The Final Act

So far I've focused on the business and technical sides of the equation. This chapter is going to deal with the spiritual side, and some of the moral issues involved in running a business. By now you're probably thinking, "I'll bet he stepped on some toes to get ahead." I have to say first, I'm not Gregg's spokesman. I can't say for sure that we never hurt anyone in a business deal, but that was surely not our intent. Let me take a moment to lay out the principles we followed in our dealings and say a few things about how we tried to conduct ourselves.

The first principle that was clear to us was that it was all God's money and He owned the business. I remember starting many meetings with prayer. It was the vision that the business existed to serve other people. It would be blessed if God chose to bless it. And we gave Him the credit when things went well.

In Gregg's view, our purpose was to help the American Farmer. Whenever we faced a tough decision, it helped to analyze it through this lens. What is best for the farmer? It's amazing how easy it is to make decisions when the main criterion is what's best for the customer. Things get really messy when you start analyzing them from the standpoint of your own bottom line, or some other weird measure. Things stay simple when you look at issues from the customer's perspective.

In the early days, we had a lot to learn. We tended to be a little too optimistic that our designs would work. So we'd get a bit carried away and sell as many as we could without sufficient testing. But you know what? We'd stand behind our product and give the customer a free product the next year as we resolved our problems. We ended up learning it was better for everyone if we did smaller-scale testing instead of swinging for the fences on the first year. But it went a long way that we took responsibility for our mistakes and tried to make things right for our customers. I remember well one of the first products that we were trying to market. It was called a PopMax plate. It required a complicated assembly, and there had already been product failure before I came to Precision. The previous season had resulted in many customers either receiving their money back or receiving the competition's parts to keep them running. So you can imagine our reaction when the first customers called this season with reports of parts coming apart in the UPS shipping. But this was an opportunity to make things right and keep a customer as happy as possible. We just started shipping out the old design of our competitors to keep things running. Yes, I'm sure in the short run it cost us some money, but in the long run, it served to build loyalty and a brand that we would capitalize on. Precision got known for getting things right in the long run and taking care of customers.

Another guiding principle was that we strove to be honest in all of our dealings. We didn't lie to suppliers to get a better quote. There is a lot of pressure on people to look at life like someone else should take the short end of the stick so that you can take the long one. Many times I've reminded others that in order to get a true picture of a situation, be it financial or otherwise, you have to draw a black box around everyone involved. This encompasses your suppliers, yourselves, and your customer. Precision didn't get ahead by cheating our suppliers. We paid them fairly and on time, so they would want to work for us in the future. One thing we noticed in our business was that we needed favors. Time was always of the essence. Getting people to do things quickly doesn't happen unless you've taken care of them in the past. We didn't lie to customers to get the sale either. We tried to just deal with others as we wanted to be dealt with. For some there's probably pressure to push the envelope and get ahead. But I'd say that you will be rewarded if you just deal honestly and fairly in everyday business.

Another one of Gregg's goals was to provide a safe workplace for the community. Safe is not real descriptive by itself, so I'll attempt to define it in the way we thought about it. I think what we meant was a workplace without fear. We wanted a workplace free from bad actions. We didn't want a workplace where people were subjected to talk and pictures they didn't like. We didn't want a workplace where employees were scared of their supervisor. We didn't want a workplace where employees were scared of their co-workers. What we wanted was a place where people felt valued, a place people wanted to come to. We wanted them to look forward to work—not as an escape from their home life, but as an escape from the normal downsides of going to "work." And I think this has been borne out by our reputation in the community. I'm not overly well-connected, but what I've heard has been positive. Production workers as well as management consider this a good company to work for. I credit Gregg's focus on employees as being the reason we've attained that.

God blessed our business greatly. But I don't think it's a coincidence. We might have been successful without following God's ways, but I tend to think that's not so. The goal in life isn't amassing wealth or being the greatest company in your field. These things may happen, but ultimately they'll only come about if you realize that God is in control, and it's all His anyway. And then live each day as though you are doing your best to serve others and help them, and decisions will be easier to sort out. It really is that simple.

Why did I call this the "final" act? We aren't living one way and then at the last minute switching. It's something we do and a way of life all along. The reason I called it final is the focus on the end. It's not about making it and ending up rich. It's about ending up in the kingdom of heaven when our life is over. This will only happen if we have served the Lord Jesus Christ and been obedient to His commands. This isn't a theological statement; it just starts with treating our employees and customers correctly.

On Monday June 30th, 2014, Derek worked a typical half day, excitedly brainstorming a future product concept with a co-worker. Later that night he started feeling worse, necessitating another trip to the hospital. Over the course of the next day he declined rapidly and on early Wednesday morning, July 2nd, in the presence of his family, he passed into eternity.

For the entire story of Derek and Leann Sauder's battle with cancer, visit their Walk of Faith blog at lrsauder.blogspot.com.

Acknowledgements

I am deeply grateful to Uncle Rich Woerner, cousin Austin Woerner, brother Doug Sauder, and sister-in-law Brooke Sauder for their many efforts on behalf of Derek. You have shared your gifts, and I am so pleased to have each of you in my life.

Thanks to Uncle Gregg and Precision Planting for creating a great place to make these experiences.

Thank you to the engineering team, customers, and suppliers who rode life's pathway with Derek, helping to inspire him in this work.

Lastly, I want to acknowledge the Giver of all good gifts, our God Almighty and His son, Jesus, who blesses us with all we need and provides a way to heaven.

Leann Sauder, wife of Derek

Made in the USA
Lexington, KY
04 May 2015